WITCHES AND GHOSTS OF PENDLE

OF PENDLE

AND THE RIBBLE VALLEY

T0323124

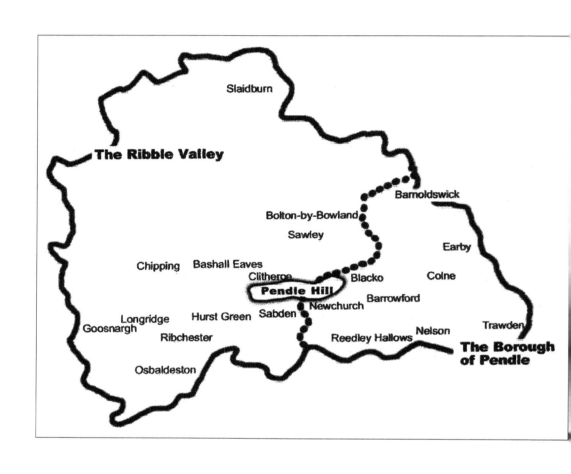

The Ribble Valley

Slaidburn

Barnoldswick

Bolton-by-Bowland

Sawley

Earby

Chipping   Bashall Eaves

Clitheroe   Blacko   Colne

Pendle Hill

Newchurch   Barrowford

Longridge   Hurst Green   Sabden   Trawden

Goosnargh

Ribchester   Reedley Hallows   Nelson

The Borough
of Pendle

Osbaldeston

WITCHES AND GHOSTS OF PENDLE AND THE RIBBLE VALLEY

JACQUELINE DAVITT

This book is dedicated to my late husband, John Davitt
(1948–2011)

Frontispiece: Map showing some of the places mentioned in
this book.

First published 2006 by Tempus Publishing

Reprinted in 2008 by
The History Press
The Mill, Brimscombe Port,
Stroud, Gloucestershire, GL5 2QG
www.thehistorypress.co.uk

Reprinted 2009, 2012

British Library Cataloguing in Publication Data.
A catalogue record for this book is available from the British Library.

ISBN 978 0 7524 4063 7

Typesetting and origination by Tempus Publishing Limited.
Printed and bound in England.

CONTENTS

ACKNOWLEDGEMENTS

Alan Billington, Christine Bradley and the helpful Lancashire librarians, Michelle Brooks, Sara Buckle, John Davitt, David Evans, Wayne Foster and Faye Medcalfe, Steven Haig, Cheryl Hindle, Pauline Holden, Brian and Ethel Jessop, Emily and Jason Keen, Irving Lawrence, Kim Lawrence, Toby Lawrence, Dawn Miller, Natasha Miller, Lawrence and Jackie Neil, Jean Peake, Barry Shepherd, Anthony Spears, Jayne Spears, Peter Smith, Dorothy Thompson, Peto Veritum, Les Walsh, Emma Watts, Eric and Mavis Wilkinson, and also my editor, David Buxton, for his help and advice.

With special thanks to Janet Cameron, who gave me the confidence to 'go for it.' Line drawings are by Kimberley Jane Lawrence and photographs by the author, unless otherwise acknowledged.

INTRODUCTION

The Borough of Pendle has a population of approximately 90,000 people and covers sixty-five square miles of Lancashire. Pressed up against the border with Yorkshire, it consists of sharply contrasting rural villages and towns that grew up in the boom years of the textile industry.

There is evidence that the borough had inhabitants long before the Industrial Revolution, with Bronze Age burial sites, an Iron Age hill fort at Castercliffe, and even a Mesolithic campsite at the foot of Boulsworth Moor. The Romans once had a foothold in the area, and the Norsemen arrived at the end of the ninth century, leaving behind them such place names as Elslack and Sough (pronounced 'Suff')

The Ribble Valley, on the other hand, has a population of about 55,000 covering one hundred and fifty square miles, about a third of which has the designation of 'area of outstanding natural beauty'. The valley has one of the lowest unemployment rates in the country, with a high level of home ownership. The countryside around Stonyhurst was probably the inspiration for J.R.R. Tolkein's 'Middle Earth', the setting of his books *The Hobbit* and *The Lord of the Rings*. The market town of Clitheroe, at the hub of the valley, has a twelfth-century Norman keep, and not far away is Ribchester, with its ruined Roman fort.

Although the boroughs of Pendle and the Ribble Valley are in some ways very different, they share an important landmark that both divides and unites their people.

This is the mysterious Pendle Hill, which stands approximately one thousand eight hundred and thirty feet at its highest point, dominating the landscape and dictating the position of towns, villages and roads for miles around. It depends on whether you live on the Pendle Borough side, or the Ribble Valley side, as to which aspect of this great mound you see every day, but the view is naturally best from the top. This is where George Fox had a vision of God in 1652, which led to his founding the Quaker movement.

As Fox stood surveying a large part of Lancashire from the windswept summit, the vastness of the view below him was so overwhelming that he later wrote in his journal ('A New Era Begins', 1652), 'From the top of this hill the Lord let me see in what places he had a great people to be gathered.'

Pendle Hill from Nogarth – The Borough of Pendle view.

Pendle Hill from the Ribble Valley.

The Ribble Valley and The Borough of Pendle also have a vast and common lore of myth and legend. They share the same witches, ghosts and boggarts, with the songs and stories of the regions both intertwining and supplementing each other.

The influence of Pendle Hill is such that it extends beyond the boundaries of the two communities, so I have included some ghostly tales from locations that are geographically just outside them, but which fall equally under the thrall of this almost-mountain.

Jacqueline Davitt.
April 2006

Old Pendle
Old Pendle, old Pendle, thou standest alone
Twixt Burnley and Clitheroe, Whalley and Colne
Where Hodder and Ribble's fair waters do meet
With Barley and Downham content at thy feet.
Old Pendle, old Pendle, o'er moorland and fell
In beauty and loveliness ever to dwell
Through life's fateful journey where'er we may be
We'll pause in our labours and oft think on thee.
Old Pendle, old Pendle – majestic, sublime
Thy praises shall ring till the end of all time
In beauty eternal thy banner unfurled
Thou dearest and grandest old hill in the world!

by Milton/Allan

I

WITCHES, GHOSTS AND BOGGARTS

WITCHES

Mention Pendle Hill to anyone and the chances are that they will reply 'Ah! The Witches!' The story of the Pendle witches and their trials was extensively recorded at the time by Thomas Potts in his 'The Wunderfull Discoverie of Witches' which gave William Harrison Ainsworth the idea for his Victorian novel *The Lancashire Witches*. In 1953, Robert Neill wrote a more modern version of the tale 'Mist over Pendle'.

The word witch comes from the Anglo-Saxon word 'Wicca' (or wicce), which is in turn derived from an ancient Indo-European word that means 'to bend, or to change'. A witch is generally accepted to be a person, often an ugly old woman, who is believed to have magical powers.

William West, an eighteenth-century English lawyer, gave this definition:

A witch or a hag is she which being deluded by a league made with the Devil through his persuasion, inspiration or juggling, thinketh she can design what manner of evil things soever, either by thought or imprecation, as to shake the air with lightenings and thunder, to cause hail and tempests, to remove green corn or trees to another place, to be carried of her familiar (which hath taken upon him the deceitful shape of a goat, swine, or calf, etc.) into some mountain far distant, in a wonderful short space of time, and sometime to fly upon a staff or fork, or some other instrument, and to show a thousand such mockeries.

An earlier definition by Reginald Scot in his 1584 manuscript 'Discoverie of Witchcraft' would perhaps be nearer the mark in describing the wretched women of Pendle who were convicted of witchcraft and hanged at Lancaster Castle in 1612.

'One sort commonly said to be witches are women which are old, lame, blear eyed, foul and full of wrinkles. Poor sullen superstitious creatures in whose drowsy minds the Devil has a fine seat!'

Typical modern image of a witch.

He goes on to tell how these women would ask for food, and if they were not given any, they would curse all and sundry. Because of the unhealthy times they lived in, eventually someone they had cursed would fall sick, or their cattle would die. Not knowing any better, the ill-educated, superstitious farmers and villagers would blame their troubles on the vengeance of the witches.

Scot continues: 'The witch on the other hand, seeing one in every hundred of her curses take effect, is convinced that she has brought misfortune to pass and confesses it. So she, her accusers and the Justices are all deceived.'

It was a local belief that a stone with a hole through it would keep witches and their spells at bay, and folk would either carry them about their person or hang them outside their cottages and farms for protection.

GHOSTS

Ghosts, spectres, spooks and phantoms are familiar concepts. They are spirits of the dead who appear in the bodily forms of once-living people and tend to haunt their former habitats. They are often silent and have no physical reality, although occasionally someone will report hearing a disembodied voice or voices whilst feeling a 'presence', or 'entity'.

BOGGARTS

There are a number of stories featuring boggarts in this book, and if you do not come from Lancashire or Yorkshire, you may not be aware of these spirits, which have their roots in the folklore of these northern counties.

Boggarts are mischievous spirits often responsible for poltergeist activity in homes and around the countryside. They sometimes attach themselves to families and may move with them from house to house. Although there are tales of them being helpful and cooperative they have an impish streak. Moving furniture, breaking cups and plates, and closing doors with a bang are all among a boggart's repertoire and they can turn malicious and nasty if they are of a mind to do so. This change in a boggart's personality is reputed to stem from many causes. The families naming the spirit, leaving him gifts – or not leaving him gifts – have all been cited, but most people agree that an angry boggart is not something they would wish upon their own homes. They can be of either sex and have the ability to alter their shape and form to appear as animals.

In some parts of the two counties, the term 'boggart' is used simply as an alternative name for a ghost.

II

A-Z BY AREA OF THE WITCHES AND GHOSTS

BARLEY

Records from 1354 show a settlement called Barleegh, meaning infertile meadow, at the foot of Pendle Hill.

In 1612, it was the home of James and John Robinson, two brothers bewitched and murdered by Alison Device, and was a regular gathering place for the Pendle witches. The oldest building in present day Barley is a seventeenth-century barn known as Wilkinson's Farm, once used as a place of worship by Irish labourers brought in to construct the local reservoirs.

The Fairy Funeral

There are myths about fairy funerals woven into the folklore of many Lancashire communities, as there are in other rural counties including Cornwall. All appear to have dire consequences for any humans that disturb the funerals and this one, told to me by a local octogenarian, is no exception.

One night towards the end of the nineteenth century, two Irish labourers who were helping build a reservoir at Black Moss decided to go out and catch a rabbit or two to supplement their rations. As they walked stealthily through Aitken Wood, they saw an eerie glow coming from a glade a little way from the path. Curious to see what was happening, they crept closer and hid behind a fallen tree trunk. To their amazement, they realised they were witnessing a fairy funeral and the light was coming from the tiny lanterns the fairies carried as they processed.

The elder of the two men motioned that they should leave at once, but the younger man had recently been involved in an argument with a fellow worker about the mortality of the 'little people' and saw an opportunity to prove his point. Leaping forward, he snatched the coffin, causing the lid to fall away. To his horror, he saw that the tiny figure lying in it was a miniature version of himself. He dropped the casket and turned to flee, but as he did so the lanterns went out and the little folk fluttered and flew in all directions. The labourer was panicking by this time and as he scrambled away, he felt sharp thorns pricking his skin and heard fairy wings flapping

Wilkinson's farm, Barley.

Did fairies once inhabit this woodland glade?

furiously about his head. Eventually, he caught up with his friend, who helped him back to their lodgings where they huddled until morning.

When it was time to go to work the younger man refused to leave his bed and when his friend returned that evening, he found him dead. The women from the village came to lay out the young labourer for burial and when they saw the myriad of tiny punctures on his skin, they shook their heads and murmured incantations over him, knowing from experience what had happened.

BARNOLDSWICK

There was a settlement at Barnoldswick during Saxon times and the town has remains of a road, which the Romans constructed, between Ribchester and Tadcaster. The Domesday Book refers to it as *Bernulfsuuic* and in 1147, a group of monks sponsored by Henry De Lacey built the church of Saint-Mary-le-Gill.

The Phantom Bomber

On 23 January 2004 the *Bradford Telegraph and Argus* reported that a couple who had been driving past Rolls Royce's Bankfield factory in Barnoldswick the previous Tuesday had seen a phantom aircraft. The couple, one of whom was a retired policewoman from Nelson, claimed to have seen a large Lancaster bomber-type plane emerging from the mist and coming straight towards them. The aeroplane had four propellers but was completely silent, and they expected it to crash into their car. When this did not happen they looked back to see if it had hit neighbouring houses, but the plane had disappeared. There were no sounds of an aircraft crashing, and no reports of a plane in distress.

Following the newspaper article, there were other 'sightings' of phantom aircraft in and around Barnoldswick and there was a revival of interest in the many stories of UFOs that had previously been spotted there. There is still a division of opinion as to whether the two phenomena have a common link.

The Spirit of the Pipes

In September 1983, a family from the Townhead area of Barnoldswick reported some strange occurrences at their home, which originally had been two separate cottages.

Three weeks after moving into the house, the male occupant woke to hear footsteps just outside the master bedroom door. Thinking it was one of the children, he got up to attend to their needs, but found they were both still soundly asleep. This happened on several consecutive nights, but it was not until some time later that the couple discovered that an old staircase had once come up just where the footsteps stopped every night.

During some renovations, the family had an impromptu music session amongst the building works. Mum banged away on some empty paint tins, her son took his violin bow and scraped a tune on a saw, whilst her husband took a spare length of copper pipe and blew into it like a trumpet. They had a good laugh at their own antics and went to bed around midnight. About an hour and a half later they woke to hear soft music but, before they had time to go downstairs to see if they had left the stereo on, it stopped. As they settled down to sleep once more, three or four blasts of the copper pipe echoed around the house, exactly as when the man had blown through it earlier that evening. No one was downstairs when the couple checked and they heard the same noise on several further occasions. They claimed that at this time they did not feel frightened or unduly concerned, even when objects seemed to move from the positions they left them in.

One evening, husband, wife, and fourteen-year-old son were eating supper when they were startled by a loud bang directly above them. They thought the bath-rack might have fallen into the bath, or a towel rail had fallen over. They went to check, but this proved not to be the case, and nothing was out of place upstairs.

The last ghostly visit to the family occurred when the woman went downstairs for a magazine at night. As she crossed the kitchen, lit only by the light from the stairs, a cold blast of air enveloped her. She ran back to bring her husband to check that no windows were open and, being somewhat unnerved by the incident, she addressed the presence saying, 'Look, if there is anything there for goodness sake show yourself, instead of playing these silly games.' Her chastisement must have worked as they never saw the ghost, or heard his phantom pipe playing, again.

BARROWFORD

Barrowford has farmhouses and weavers' cottages that date back to the seventeenth and eighteenth centuries.

Address to Barrowford:

Dear Vale of my ancestors, sweet Barrowford,
With Local Board sages and dapper School Board,
The village of wisdom and learning profound,
Where palaces, fair and historic, abound;
Dar vale of my childhood, dear forest of fame,
Whence mystery deep, and mythology came,
The legends that hang round the forester's home
Are rich as the fables of Greece, or of Rome.
Henry Nutter (1892)

The Lamb Club

Thomas and Grace Sutcliffe built the Lamb Working Men's Club in the centre of Barrowford, in 1696 and it is one of the oldest remaining buildings in the village. The last Sutcliffe lived at Bank Hall, as it was then called, until 1857, but it remained a 'gentleman's residence' until the Working Men's Institute bought the building in 1904 for the sum of £587 10s 6d.

Considering the building's age, it is not surprising that many members down the years have reported feeling 'a presence' at the club. The eerie feeling has mainly centred on the wood-panelled committee room, or on the stairs leading to it, where people have felt something brushing past them. The earliest stories seem to relate to the unused room over the bar area, which is now blocked off, but was once the accommodation for the club's stewards and their families. However, the snooker room, which constituted the major part of the club in its early years, has been the focus of more recent phenomena.

In the early 1990s, the late, much respected club treasurer, Tommy Kelly, was working in the committee room with the secretary, Irving Lawrence, just before evening opening time. As usual, they had locked all the doors behind them, so were surprised to hear the sounds of a snooker game in progress in the room beneath. The clink of the balls was familiar to both men so they went to investigate only to find the snooker table empty, as was the club, with the door locks still firmly in place.

Right: Doorway of the Lamb Club, showing date stone of 1696.

Below: The scene of a ghostly snooker game at the Lamb Club.

Irving, feeling somewhat unnerved by this, made a joke about it being 'a ghost' to which Tommy replied that it was not the first incident of its kind that he had witnessed during his many years as a member.

A more recent secretary, Steven Haig, told me that he has been alone in the building when appliances have seemingly turned themselves on or off and the music system has suddenly sprung into life.

No one appears to know who the ghost may have been and old stories of Barrowford make no mention of Bank Hall being haunted before its conversion to a club, so the consensus is that it is more likely to be the spirit of a past member than that of a more ancient inhabitant.

The Pedlar's Ghost

In Jesse Blakey's 1929 book *The Annals of Barrowford*, he recounts the story of a pedlar, Old Solomon, who peddled his wares around the Pendle area.

One day, a group of ruffians attacked Old Solomon and robbed him of his valuable stock. They killed him and incinerated his body in an oven, so depriving him of a burial in consecrated ground. The attack took place near the bottom of Halstead Lane, where a cotton mill now stands, but in those days, it was an open space through which ran a clough, or sluice. Years later a man found a body in the clough and the villagers attributed this murder to the pedlar's ghost, who they thought was still roaming the area to seek his revenge. Parents would warn their offspring not to venture out after dark or 'Old Solomon will get you.'

In the 1950s, nine-year-old Dorothy Parr went on an errand to a relative's house that was further up the village, and had to pass close to this spot. Dusk was falling and the young girl was running along, eager to deliver her message so that she could return to the fireside. As she dashed

Council offices at the bottom of Halstead Lane, Barrowford, near to where 'Old Solomon' was murdered.

past the wood yard and towards Bankhouse Street, she was aware of a figure swiftly approaching from the opposite direction. Dorothy swerved out into the street to avoid the impending collision and felt a waft of cold air as they passed. She turned quickly to see who was in such a hurry, but the street was empty. Dorothy still wonders to this day, if she had a close encounter with Old Solomon that night.

BASHALL EAVES

Near to the small hamlet of Bashall Eaves is a bridge known as the 'Fairy Bridge.' The Little Folk supposedly erected the bridge overnight to help an old woodcutter escape from a coven of bloodthirsty witches.

Jim Dawson's Ghost

Bashall Eaves is a long established village community situated about five miles from Clitheroe. The story of Jim Dawson's ghost goes back to 1934, when John, a middle-aged bachelor who lived with his sister, was returning to their farm after his usual Sunday evening visit to the local pub.

As the farmer reached home and turned to shut the gate, he felt something hit his back. He thought that someone had thrown a stone at him, but could not see anyone hanging about and, perhaps due to his alcohol intake, he ate his supper and went to bed as normal.

During the night, the pain in his back worsened, and when morning came, John asked his sister to see what the problem was. His sister found a gaping wound running down the left hand side of his back, and sent for the doctor. The doctor contacted the police and ambulance services, but the unfortunate farmer died three days later in Blackburn Royal Infirmary. At the inquest, the Coroner revealed that a bullet had killed Jim Dawson and that it was homemade.

The police questioned every local gun owner and searched every tool shed and workshop in the area, but all to no avail. No motive for the murder was ever established, and not a single clue turned up to aid the police in their enquiries.

The hunt for a solution to the killing seems to have only one continuing investigator – the ghost of the farmer himself. Jim Dawson's ghost still wanders the lanes, searching the hedges around his farm as though looking for clues. He wears the torn coat that he wore on his last visit to the pub, and the wound in his back still oozes blood.

The Curse of the Skull

The Parker family have lived at Browsholme Hall, near Clitheroe, since Edmund Parker built the original red sandstone house in 1507.

During renovation work in the early eighteenth century, workers found a skull on the top floor. Believing it to be a relic of a martyr from the Pilgrimage of Grace, the Parkers resited the ghoulish memento in the family chapel. The skull was treated with due respect until the mid-nineteenth century, when a young Edward Parker decided to play a joke on his family and buried it in the garden.

A series of deaths and disasters then befell the Parkers: fires started mysteriously about the house and estate and the fabric of the hall began to crumble away. Eventually Edward admitted what he had done and the family dug up the skull and returned it to the hall for safekeeping.

Nowadays the skull is locked in an ancient box that came from Ingleton Hall and is not moved from the house, or shown to strangers – just in case!

BLACKO

Blacko lies on the old turnpike road to Gisburn and its famous tower, which looks as though it belongs to medieval times, was in reality built as a folly in 1890 by local grocer Jonathan Stansfield.

The Farmer's Dog

The Cross Gaits Inn, which is reputed to be over a thousand years old, stands on a strategic corner just outside the village of Blacko. It was used as a rest stop for mail coaches in years gone by, when prisoners often accompanied coaches from other parts of Lancashire and Yorkshire on their way to the dungeons of Lancaster castle, and the place where most of the Pendle witches met their end.

Some of the chains used to tether the felons outside the inn whilst their guards took refreshment are still in evidence by the main door, where there are also iron rings through which they would pass ropes to help pull the coaches up the steep incline in the road. The cottages across the road from the inn were formerly livery stables that supplied fresh horses for the onward journey.

Peter Smith, who has been landlord of the Cross Gaits since late 2000, is of the opinion that it is his pub rather than those often cited in Barley and Downham that was the regular haunt of the Pendle witches. He told me that the remains of Malkin Tower, a favourite meeting place for the coven, are in a field at the rear of his building, pointing out that it was quite a distance from the Pendleside pub where the authorities supposedly arrested one of the witches. Blacko village folklore places that event at the Cross Gaits.

Although the inn has such a long, eventful, history, its ghosts seem to be from a more modern era. Peter described how his customers have seen the ghost of a collie curled under a bench by the fireplace.

Blacko Tower, built as a folly, looms over the village.

Right: Cross Gaits Inn sign, depicting a witch and a traveller, with Malkin Tower in the background.

Below: The Cross Gaits Inn, Blacko.

The dog, which belonged to an old farmer who frequented the pub, is supposedly waiting for the cleaner to finish her chores and take him home, just as she used to do almost every day during the 1940s and early 1950s. Customers have also reported seeing the cleaner herself, perched on a stool at the end of the bar. She is dressed in the clothes of the times and wears her hair up in a bun.

Over the entrance to the inn, there is an old sign that reads, 'Good Ale Tomorrow for Nothing'. This jovial motto was placed there by John Singlehurst in 1736 and has persuaded many a hopeful, if not so bright, passer-by to return the next day – only, of course, to be greeted by the same message.

BOLTON-BY-BOWLAND

The Domesday Book refers to the ancient village of Bolton-by-Bowland as 'Bodeton'. One of the two greens at its centre still sports a thirteenth-century market cross and a set of stocks used, in days gone by, for the punishment of local criminals and ne'er-do-wells.

Bolton Hall

King Henry VI hid at Bolton Hall, the ancestral home of the Pudsay family, following his defeat at the battle of Hexham in 1464.

Sir Ralph Pudsay, the squire at this time, had twenty-five children by three wives, and his magnificent tomb in the parish church of St Peter and St Paul depicts the knight, his head resting on two deer, flanked by his wives Matilda, Margaret and Edwina. Inscribed on each of the women's dresses is the number of children that they bore.

A later owner of Bolton Hall, William Pudsay, spent most of the Pudsay fortune on a fancy lifestyle and in payment of fines for the family's non-attendance at church. He was near to ruin when he encountered a group of fairies in a woodland glade on his land. They gave him a magical silver bit, which they claimed would give his horse great strength and stamina without the need for food, telling the astonished William that they had found the silver in his lead mine near Rimmington. The squire's men dug further into the mine and discovered a rich lode of the metal, which William turned into coins (known as the Pudsay shillings) at his own mint. The Royal Mint eventually heard about this and sent soldiers to Bolton Hall to arrest him, but William harnessed his horse with the magic bit and by making a spectacular leap down a ninety-foot precipice at Rainsber Scar, he escaped to London where Queen Elizabeth pardoned him.

Bolton Hall was demolished in the mid-twentieth century, but in its heyday in the late nineteenth century, it was open to the public who went there to see a display of three macabre skeletons. These were the bones of a horse called Balloon Boy, a Frenchman and a hound called Milton Spanker. The Hall also had a 'ghost room' during this time, but which of the many colourful Pudsays once haunted their ancestral home is something of a mystery.

BRIERFIELD

Brierfield, lying midway between Nelson and Burnley, has a strong Quaker tradition.

An early Meeting House was at the centre of the village in days gone by, and a bridge on the road towards Fence has long had the name of 'The Quaker Bridge'.

The stocks and thirteenth-century market cross at Bolton-by-Bowland.

Brierfield centre in days gone by. (courtesy of Lancashire County Library and Information Services)

Quaker Bridge. (courtesy of Lancashire County Library and Information Services)

The Ghost in a Flat Cap

The Wagon and Horses public house has been a watering hole for Brierfield's working men for many years. In December of 2000, the *Nelson Leader* ran a story about a newly installed landlord, David Mayer, and his encounters with the pub's ghost.

Mr Mayer told the *Leader* how, since moving in a few weeks previously, he had heard doors banging, glasses smashing, and things falling to the floor. However, when the new landlord went to investigate these noises, he found all was in order and that he was alone in the building.

The regulars at the Wagon and Horses confirmed that they too had witnessed odd things happening there over the years. One customer had told Mr Mayer how there used to be two jugs hanging on hooks behind the bar, which would start banging together when no one was near them. The hooks were spaced too far apart for anyone to be able to bang the jugs together manually, although many had tried. Although they did not give the ghost a name, they claimed he was an old man who walked with a stoop, wore a flat cap, and always sat at the same corner table.

The Rocking Granny

In the mid 1980s, Rob and Jenny needed to move to Pendle from the Midlands because of Rob's new promotion at work. They had already bought a house in the Reedley area when Rob started his new job, but a problem with renovations at the couple's new home meant that it would be a few weeks before they could move in.

One of Rob's new colleagues told him that his grandmother had died quite recently and the house was up for sale, but offered them the use of it until their own house was habitable.

Preferring this idea to hotel accommodation or a long daily commute, Rob accepted the keys and took his wife to see the terraced cottage on one of Brierfield's oldest streets.

Odds and ends of furniture were still dotted around the house, including a rickety wooden rocking chair in front of the living room fireplace. The couple wandered round, deciding that the cottage would be fine for a few weeks and discussing what furniture they would need to get out of storage. As they were about to go back downstairs, Rob needed to visit the bathroom, so Jenny continued down by herself. As she walked through the kitchen, she had a partial view of the living room and saw an old woman rocking in the fireside chair. The woman had her face turned away and was wearing a grey headscarf.

Embarrassed and confused, thinking that the woman had wandered in from the street or that they were inspecting the wrong house, Jenny dashed back for Rob, who she met on the stairs. She explained what she had seen and the couple swiftly returned to the living room.

The chair was empty, but moving gently on its worn rockers. The door was on the latch, and nothing had been disturbed.

Next day Rob told his colleague what they had witnessed. The man went pale and had to sit down. He told Rob that his granny, who had worn a headscarf since her hair had started to thin several years before, had sat for hours in the old rocking chair in front of the fire.

Jenny and Rob had a word with their builder and decided that they would move into their own house, which he would finish renovating with them *in situ*.

BURNLEY

The industrial town of Burnley lies at the confluence of two rivers, the Calder and the Brun. It edges onto the Borough of Pendle, with which it shares a bus service, a large chunk of heritage, and Pendle Hill.

A Bloodthirsty Boggart

Long before Turf Moor, home of the Clarets, came into existence the area at the bottom of Brunshaw was a wild and overgrown place with several streams that criss-crossed on their way to the rivers Brun and Calder.

A local bus - one in a series bearing witches' names.

A bloodthirsty boggart once inhabited the region, known as 'The Bee Hole'. This creature had a habit of waylaying travellers and either drowning them in the streams or leading them to some other grisly death. One night the boggart surpassed himself when he came upon an old woman who was reputedly a witch. An argument ensued in which they threatened and cursed each other, until the boggart overcame the old hag and killed her. He took her body away for his own evil purposes, but left her skin hanging from a thorn bush as a warning to all who would cross him.

For many years, a stand at the football ground bore the title of 'The Bee Hole End', but this was knocked down in the 1990s and replaced with the Jimmy McIlroy Stand, which many supporters still tend to refer to by its older, more evocative name.

The Boggart in a Ball-Gown

Rowley Hall, the long-time home of the Halstead family, was also once home to a female boggart. This rather grand lady-boggart used to appear to the occupants of the hall dressed in a beautiful, and elaborate, ball-gown.

Whether the lady in question died wearing her finery on the evening of a ball is not clear, nor do there appear to be any clues to her past identity, but it seems that something displeased her because her mischievousness was quite forceful. When this boggart was about doors would fly open and slam shut again without apparent reason, whilst at other times they would be stuck fast preventing the household from functioning as normal.

As tradition dictates, the well-dressed boggart was eventually 'layed' and a large stone was set in the ground to mark the rite, and to seal the boggart securely in the spirit world. This stone is still visible near to where two streams converge just below Rowley Hall.

General Scarlett

General James Yorke Scarlett commanded The Heavy Brigade at the battle of Balaclava during the Crimean war. A sensible, well-liked leader, his job was to smash through enemy lines. He rode with his six hundred men into the thick of the battle, somehow surviving against great odds to emerge practically unscathed, apart from a deep dint in his brass helmet.

He married a Burnley woman, settling at Bank Hall, on the edges of what is now Thompson Park, and after his death in 1871, his family buried the general at Holme Chapel. His ghost, dressed in full dress uniform (appropriately scarlet in colour) and mounted on a white charger supposedly walks around the old fence-line of his property during the autumn, when mists rise and swirl along the nearby riverbank.

The Phantom Printer

Whenever the printing press, or its related machinery, breaks down at the *Burnley Express* Office in Bull Street, someone will blame the mishap on 'Old Ned.'

A former colleague, whose overseer he had been whilst still alive, first saw old Ned in the 1930s. Ned's real name was Edward Fishpool, a native of Middlesborough who had come to the area in 1909 and joined the *Burnley Express* in 1910 to work as a printer.

He was a loyal and willing employee, and was very proud when his bosses asked him to supervise the removal of his old machinery to Nottinghamshire. This was a very tricky task, so Ned was determined to make sure that all went well but, shortly before the move was to take place, he contracted pneumonia and was unable to complete the job.

A few days after the machinery removal took place without his help, Ned succumbed to his illness and died, still upset that he had been unable to fulfil his obligations.

The phantom printer is still occasionally seen moving through the offices or, more usually, on the machine room balcony.

The Saxon Cross and the Demon Pigs

The Saxon cross that now stands in the grounds of the old Grammar school at the corner of School Lane and Colne Road, not far from Burnley's town centre, used to dominate the bottom of Godly lane, near to Ormerod Road. Tradition has it that its old position marked the spot where St Paulinus baptised most of his local converts to Christianity in the River Brun.

Tradition also has it that this holy site was where the devout Christians of Burnley decided to build their first parish church. Every night during the construction work, demon pigs supposedly pulled down the walls that the builders had laid during the day, carrying the stones away to the site on which the church still stands, preventing the holy spot blessed by St Paulinus from having a special significance.

There is a carving of what looks like a pig hewn roughly into the south side of the church, which may substantiate the legend, but it is just as likely to be the more Christian symbol of a lamb, which the combination of weather and soot deposits from the old mill chimneys have gradually worn away.

The Saxon cross in the grounds of the old grammar school, Burnley.

A Presence at St Peter's

In September 2003, the induction of a new rector, known to his parishioners as 'Canon Bill' took place at St Peter's church, Burnley. Ethel Jessop, an enrolling member, asked her husband Brian to video the proceedings so he took himself off to a vantage point in a room on the top floor of the building.

Brian, a retired joiner, closed the door of the room behind him and began filming through the window. He was concentrating on getting some good footage, when he heard the door open and bang shut again, followed by someone tapping his shoulder. Brian turned to tell whoever it was trying to attract his attention that he would be with them in a moment, but the room was empty and the door still firmly closed. Brian admits to being 'spooked' by the incident, but he told me he did not feel afraid.

His experience did not surprise Alan Billington, who has been the churchwarden at St Peter's for many years, as he confirmed that he too had sensed a ghostly presence in the building on more than one occasion. Alan's most recent sighting took place during a church service in 2005 when, because of his duties, he was sitting on the back row of pews. He said that he saw a woman suddenly appear in the nave and walk across the church towards the far aisle. She was dressed all in white, which Alan thought unusual, but he had the impression that her attire was of the era. He got up and walked in the same direction to see if the woman was all right, but could not see her in the congregation or in any of the side areas. Alan knew that she had not passed him to go out of the main door and he described how the hair on the back of his neck 'stood on end'. No one else in the church that day saw the lady in white, or knew who she might be.

St Peter's church, Burnley: the haunt of a lady in white.

The Satan Spell

The Old Grammar school stands next to the Burnley parish church of St Peter, and is now a crèche for the College of Further Education. There is a legend surrounding it, which succeeding generations of students have adopted as their own, but which actually dates back to the time when the building was a Grammar school for boys.

It appears that some of the scholars discovered an old book in the school library, which described spells, charms, and incantations. The Harry Potter spirit being present in boys even then, they were curious about the effectiveness of these spells, especially the one that claimed to enable the chanter to raise Satan from his lair in Hell.

They waited until no teachers were around before trying out the spell, and one particularly brave lad agreed to read out the incantations. The final part of the ritual required the boy to read the Lord's Prayer backwards, which he did with great gusto. As he finished the chant with a theatrical flourish of his arms into the air the gathering was amazed and terrified to see one of the flagstones beneath them tilt and spring up, followed by the coal-black horned head of the Devil popping up through the hole. The horrified pupils panicked, and seizing any hard objects that came to hand, they pounded the repulsive figure until it retreated, howling, to wherever it had come from.

A strange black mark still exists on the flagstone marking the spot where this event is reputed to have taken place.

The old grammar school, Burnley where pupils raised the Devil with a spell.

A Ghostly Musician

There have been several reports of ghostly hands playing the piano in the lecture theatre of Burnley Central Library.

The first report came from a librarian who was working alone after the library had closed for the evening, when he heard classical music coming from the room above. He went to investigate, and found the lecture room empty whilst the piano was playing of its own accord.

The ghostly pianist has never manifested itself whilst producing its beautiful music, but one suggestion is that it may be a soul emanating from one of the old houses that previously stood on the site of the library.

CHIPPING

The Domesday Book has a record of Chipping, and the village is reputedly over a thousand years old, so it is not surprising that it should harbour a ghost or two.

Lizzie Dean

Lizzie Dean was a young girl who worked as a serving wench at the Sun Inn on Windy Street. She was engaged to a local lad and was looking forward to being married in the near future. The bride to be was in her room at the inn one day when she heard the church bells ringing.

Looking across the street to see what the occasion was, she saw her fiancé, dressed in his Sunday best, walking down the church path having just married another girl.

Lizzie was, naturally, distraught at this and could not be consoled. She hanged herself soon afterwards, leaving a suicide note in which she asked that they bury her beneath that same path, so that her cruel fiancé would have to walk across her grave every time he attended services. The vicar refused to allow this and interred her body at the southeast corner of the church instead. Because of this lack of respect for her last wishes, Lizzie refused to leave the Sun Inn, where the abandoned bride's spectre still appears from time to time.

Customers there claim to have seen Lizzie's ghost drift from the stairs that lead to her bedroom and hover around the snooker area. She is dressed in her old-fashioned uniform and has a tendency to disappear through the walls. They say that doors creak without reason in the pub and that glasses swing on their hooks when nobody is near them.

Local children in Chipping still carry out an old tradition of tying shut the church gates following a wedding, so that the bride and groom have to toss coins to them in order to leave. Whether this custom has anything to do with the Lizzie Dean tragedy is a matter of opinion, with some locals linking the two, whilst others claim that the tradition predates Lizzie's death and still takes place in some of the surrounding villages.

Leagram Hall

George Weld practically rebuilt Leagram Hall, the ancient seat of the Shireburns, in 1822. He also added the Gothic chapel of St Mary in 1856.

In 1963, more major alterations took place resulting in some badly buried bodies being uncovered and re-interred at St Mary's church. This seemed to trigger some spirit activity and *The Clitheroe Advertiser and Times* of 19 April 1963 carried a report of how passengers driving past the old Keeper's cottage had witnessed the grey ghost of an old man rising from the road in front of their car, before disappearing into the night.

In December 1974, the same newspaper told how Joe and Valerie Huddleston, and their seven-year-old daughter Joan, were being troubled by bumping and banging in the room above, as they sat around the fireside in their cottage at the rear of the hall. They too suspected that the spirits of those souls disturbed by building work at the Hall had returned to haunt them.

The locals have grown used to 'spooky' tales surrounding Leagram Hall, but some of them are still inclined to give the area a wide birth on dark nights.

CLAYTON-LE-MOORS

Clayton-Le-Moors derives its name from the 'clay town on the moors' because of the countless bricks it has provided to build houses throughout the area.

Lucette

The first record of Dunkenhalgh is from 1285, although it may have existed for some time prior to this date. The Rishton family, who gave their name to the nearby village in which they originally lived, owned the house for over two hundred years from 1332 onwards. It is now a hotel and conference centre.

Christmas Eve, at midnight, the ghost of Lucette, a French governess employed by the Petre family in the eighteenth century, reputedly walks the grounds. She wears a white sheet-like garment and glides beneath the leafless trees next to the bridge, where she then disappears.

Lucette had the misfortune to fall in love with, and become pregnant by, a handsome army officer. He promised to marry the mademoiselle after his current campaign finished, but he did not come back to Clayton-Le-Moors to honour his word. Because of her condition, the young governess did not dare to return to her family home in France and began to wander despairingly around the glades she had frequented with her lover. One night, finally overwhelmed by grief and worry, she threw herself from the bridge into the freezing waters of the River Hyndburn, where she perished.

A year later, her lover returned to Dunkenhalgh where Lucette's brother, blaming the young officer for his sister's death, challenged him to a duel and killed him.

Lucette still makes a yearly return to the grounds of The Dunkenhalgh Hotel to see if her beloved has returned to claim her as his bride, but it appears that they have yet to meet in the afterlife.

CLITHEROE

The busy market town of Clitheroe and the surrounding countryside hold plenty of ghostly secrets, from river sprites to howling dogs. Its castle, perched precariously on a limestone outcrop overlooking the town, still has a standing keep, which was a Royalist garrison during the Civil war.

Peg O'Nell

According to local legend, Peg O'Nell was a servant girl who worked for the Starkie family at their Tudor mansion, Waddow Hall, during the eighteenth century. The house, currently owned by the Guide's Association, stands in a hundred and seventy-eight acres of parkland on the banks of the river Ribble.

One day, Peg had a row with her employer, (and some say reputed witch), who then sent her to collect water from the well, calling after her '…And I hope you break your neck!' Peg never returned, but her malicious spirit still haunts the shallow rectangular well where she reputedly met her end. The legend says that Peg's curse on the hall and its occupant's demands that the family must sacrifice a living creature every seven years. If a dog, cat or some other domestic animal does not die, then Peg will return to extract her revenge, and will claim a human victim by drowning.

Standing by the well is a headless female statue, possibly a figure of St Margaret, which may have originated from a religious building, dismantled during the bitter quarrels of the Reformation. The statue acquired the sacrilegious title of 'Meg', which later became 'Peg', and came to represent, and to take the blame for, all the ills that befell the locals. Mistress Starkie of Waddow Hall, following the near drowning of a puritan preacher in the River Ribble, eventually beheaded the figure. Some say that the curse will be broken if the head is found, and reunited with its body.

Peg sometimes appears as a dark-hooded figure gliding through the grounds, or mounting the stairs to her bedroom from where the sound of her footsteps still echo through the hall from time to time.

The Dule upo' Dun

No book about strange happenings in Pendle and the Ribble Valley would be complete without the story of 'The Dule Upo' Dun'. Whilst it has no witches, ghosts, or boggarts, it illustrates the inhabitants' ability to triumph over the Devil and so merits inclusion.

Clitheroe Castle.

Waddow Hall, where Peg O'Nell worked as a servant.

'The Dule Upo' Dun' was an old inn, no longer standing, that had a sign illustrating its unusual name. It depicted a furious Satan riding bareback on a dun coloured horse, watched by a small, happy-looking tailor. The tailor in the picture was not always so happy; in fact, he used to be a drunkard who spent all his money on ale, while his wife did menial work to put food on the table.

One night he was drinking with his cronies when a stranger, dressed in sombre black and carrying a gold-topped cane, joined them in their revelry. The tailor's money ran out before his thirst was slaked, and when the Landlord refused him credit, he left in a furious temper. The stranger caught up with him on the road and told him of a way to become rich by making a pact with the Devil. The tailor was so desperate for money that he accepted his offer, whereupon the man in black incanted the Pater Noster (The Lord's Prayer) backwards to conjure up his master.

When Satan appeared, the tailor was

The headless statue of Peg O'Nell stands besides an old well.

so terrified that he tried to back out of the deal but Satan warned him that he must either go with him to Hell that night, or sign an agreement whereby he would get three wishes for himself and his wife in exchange for surrendering his soul in seven years time. The tailor took the latter option and signed the agreement with blood pricked from his finger.

He rushed home to tell his wife, but as he walked through the door, she was putting his meal of porridge on the table and greeted him saying, 'I wish I had a collop of bacon for ye'. Instantly a rasher of bacon appeared on his plate and the tailor, realising one wish had gone, ranted at his poor wife shouting, 'Woman, I wish that thou wert far away.' At this, of course, his long-suffering spouse disappeared.

Left alone, the tailor's lifestyle deteriorated and eventually, when he could stand no more, he used his last wish to bring his wife back. United with his wife, the tailor saw the error of his ways, stopped drinking, and began to earn a good living.

By the end of the seven years, he was quite well to do, but knowing that the Devil would soon be coming to claim his soul he sought advice from a wise monk who gave him the benefit of his holy knowledge. When Satan appeared, the tailor was ready for him and taunted him, saying that Old Nick had tricked him into signing the agreement and he did not believe that he actually had the power to make him rich. The Devil was unused to people challenging him, so he arrogantly told the mere mortal that he would prove his might by granting him one last wish. The wily tailor pointed at a horse in a nearby field and cried, 'I wish thou wert riding back to thy quarters on yon dun horse, and never able to plague me again'. Thunder and lightening cracked the sky, and unseen hands picked Satan up and hurled him onto the animals back, whereupon the dun horse galloped off, with its rider screaming foul abuse and curses as he clung to its mane.

Some years later, relatives of the tailor and his wife opened the inn with money left to them by the childless couple and named it 'The Dule Upo' Dun' (the Devil on a dun horse) in respect to their benefactors' story.

The Bloodstained Bridge

During Clitheroe's March Fair in 1773, a group of ruffians murdered a local man, George Battersby, on the bridge in Waddington Road. Following the killing, the perpetrators moved the body from place to place in an attempt to evade detection. In 1776, some boys from the Grammar School found Battersby's decayed remains in the churchyard bone house.

Although the badly decomposed body made identification practically impossible, the constables arrested three men and tried them for the crime in April 1778. After a trial lasting many hours, the court acquitted them due to lack of evidence, but the citizens of Clitheroe had already decided that they were guilty and ostracised those concerned.

Over the years, George Battersby's ghost has appeared regularly, gliding over the bridge and disappearing through the hedge. Some of the older townspeople still believe that his blood appears on part of the bridge's stonework during the month of March each year. There are rumours too, of other ghostly figures, presumably the murderers, moving furtively around the ditch in which they first concealed his body, and there is supposedly a patch in the nearby hedge where the vegetation has never grown back.

Trash

Clitheroe has its own version of a dog-like animal with saucer eyes that is similar in description to other Lancashire boggarts. This one, whom the locals call 'Trash', had connections with The Old Hall, a long-demolished building that stood between Fishergate and Castlegate.

A sighting of 'Trash' was supposed to herald the observer's death, or that of a close family member.

CLIVIGER

Three miles southeast of Burnley, the village of Cliviger lies in a rugged gorge of the same name.

The White Doe and the Huntsman

On All Hallows Eve, at a desolate spot near to Eagle's Crag, the spectre of a beautiful white doe runs for her life. Behind her, in hot pursuit, chase a ghostly huntsman and his pack of baying hounds.

Lady Sybil lived in a small, fortified house, known as Bernshaw Tower, which stood several miles outside Burnley in Cliviger Gorge. She was not only beautiful and extremely wealthy, but she had an intelligent interest in biology, botany and the mysticism of nature. The high-born lady longed to become a member of the Pendle witch coven and struck a deal with the Devil in which she exchanged her soul for his promise that all her wishes would be granted.

The Lady Sybil was not the only member of her circle to enlist the forces of evil to achieve their ambitions: She had a suitor, Lord William Towneley of nearby Hapton Tower, who turned to a local witch, known as Mother Helston, after Sybil had refused his many offers of marriage. The hag agreed to help Lord William, and after collecting due payment she incanted a spell, designed to ensure that his pursuit of his loved one would come to fruition on the next All Hallows' Eve.

Eagle's Crag: the witch's perch.

On the appointed night, Lady Sybil was cavorting around her beloved Eagle's Crag in the form of a white doe, when William and his hunting dogs confronted her. The pack included a large slavering hound, which legend says was Mother Helston's familiar. The white doe led the pack a merry chase around the rocky countryside, but they eventually cornered her on the edge of a precipice. Mother Helston's familiar grabbed her neck in its huge jaws, holding the struggling animal until Lord William tethered his prize with a magical silken rope.

The triumphant lord took the doe to Hapton, where a storm arose in the night, buffeting and shaking the tower, as though the Devil was angry at the capture of one of his promised souls. Lord William summoned Mother Helston once more, and she managed to intervene and release Lady Sybil from her pact with Satan. Lady Sybil reverted to her usual appearance and married Lord William, the couple settling at Hapton Tower.

Unfortunately, their married bliss did not last for long, and Sybil again took up her supernatural practices. One night she adopted the form of a large white cat in order to prowl around a nearby flourmill, where a guard spotted her and cut off her paw. Next day William discovered his wife bleeding from the stump of her wrist. A servant found his mistress' severed hand and with yet more help from Mother Halston they managed to re-attach it to her arm. Notwithstanding, it soon became apparent that Lady Sybil was dying and she confessed her sins, hoping to cancel out her obligation to the Devil.

At Halloween the spirit of the ill-fated Lady Sybil and her husband, William, meet once again to re-enact the thrill of the chase.

The Boggart of Barcroft Hall

Barcroft Hall is a farmhouse, which dates from 1614, according to the date inscribed over an inner entrance. It stands off Park Avenue in Cliviger, just outside Burnley, and was a magnificent building during the fifteenth, sixteenth, and seventeenth centuries.

The legend of the Barcroft boggart stretches back to when the hall was a busy working farmhouse. The tale says that at one time he was a friendly amiable boggart, who would not only help with the general farm chores, but would have the household's washing and ironing finished before the family woke up in the mornings.

One evening, heavy snow began to fall after the farmer and his wife had gone to bed. The farmer shouted to his sons that they should take the sheep into the barn, where they would be warmer. Instead of a reply from his sons, he heard a squeaky voice call out, 'I'll do it, I'll do it'. The farmer waited, and in a short while, the same voice shouted, 'I've done, I've done, but I had trouble with the small brown 'un'.

When the farmer went to check his flock the next morning, he found a large brown hare in amongst the flock and chuckled at the boggart's mistake.

The farmer and the boggart continued in this friendly vein, until one of the farmer's sons decided to reward the old spirit for his helpful ways. He made him a pair of wooden clogs, and left them by the hearth where the boggart would be sure to find them.

Now, some legends have it that a boggart can do no harm until he receives a gift and this appears to be true in this case, as the presentation of the clogs seemed to bring about a change in this one's personality. He became mischievous and downright malicious at times. He began to fling pots and pans around the kitchen, causing havoc, and breaking the farmer's wife's best candlesticks and nick-nacks in the process. Animals suddenly became lame, or died, and hens stopped laying eggs. The chaos reached a climax one day when the farmer woke to the sound of clattering above his head, and found his prize bull on the farmhouse roof.

He decided then that the family had endured enough of the boggart's antics and loaded his household belongings onto his cart ready to move out of his home. As the cart began to trundle down the lane the boggart's voice squeaked out, 'Stop theer, while I tee mi' clogs, an' I'll go with thee!'

The farmer realised the futility of trying to escape from the old spirit and returned to Barcroft.

There does not appear to be an ending, happy or otherwise, to the legend. So whether the boggart's behaviour improved or the family learned to live with his mischief you will have to decide for yourself.

The Witch of Eagle's Crag

During the reign of Charles I, a witch terrorised travellers on the road between Burnley and Todmorden. Her favourite perch was atop Eagle's Crag where she could look down on all who passed along the valley floor.

One All Saints Day, a farmer called Giles Robinson was travelling along this route late at night after his business in town had taken him longer than he had anticipated. As he approached Eagle's Crag, he heard an almighty crash in the air around him, and a fork of lightening hit the ground where he was just about to step. He looked up towards where the lightening had seemed to come from and saw the witch astride the rocky outcrop at the very summit of the crag. The lightening appeared to emanate from her up-stretched arms and the farmer watched, mesmerised by the sight, as heavy rain began to fall and the valley echoed with rumbling thunder.

Giles jerked from his stupor and ran blindly on seeking shelter but, in his panic, he stumbled over something that crossed his path. He found himself confronted by a hissing black cat with fiery red eyes, which then turned around and ran screeching up the crag side. The frightened man watched as the cat jumped onto the witch's shoulder and the pair flew through the sky together in the direction of Pendle Hill.

Despite the driving rain and the fierce lightening, Giles started to run and continued running until he reached his farmhouse, where he told his wife what had happened and predicted that this ill omen meant that a tragedy would occur in the near future.

The desolate area around Eagle's Crag, where Lady Sybil was captured in the form of a white doe.

COLNE

The ancient market town of Colne has a church with parts dating back to the eleventh century. It is also the birthplace of Wallace Arnold, the bandmaster of the Titanic, whose statue stands on the town's main thoroughfare.

Colne Hall

In 1976, a local newspaper report told how workers at the Princess of Norway curtaining company in Linden Road, Colne regularly heard ghostly footsteps coming from an empty room. Some of the machinists said they could feel a 'presence' and one woman claimed to have actually seen the ghost.

The earliest records of Colne Hall are of Robert Shaw building it as a manor house in the middle of the nineteenth century. It later became a beer hall before the co-operative movement bought it for retail premises in 1903. After the Norwegian curtain company left the premises, it became a housing complex.

Tony Halstead interviewed a former caretaker of the building, Fred Pearson, who said he was not at all surprised by these new revelations. Mr Pearson claimed that he had always felt a presence as he worked alone at night, and had once seen the ghost of a young girl as he was stoking the boiler. He said the girl was dressed in old-fashioned clothes and had told him that she had come 'to see if the cinders were all right' before vanishing. There was a fierce fire in the building sometime later, and some people wondered if the girl had appeared in an effort to forewarn them.

Mr Pearson had two large dogs that were frightened to enter one particular upstairs room and he had heard footsteps coming from there when no one else was in the building.

This seems to corroborate machinists' experiences and local belief in the Hall's ghost.

Colne Hall.

Colne parish church.

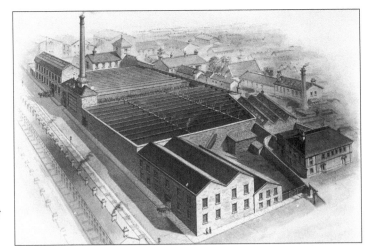

The ghost at Frankland's mill showed an interest in modern technology. (courtesy of Lancashire Library and Information Services)

Colne Parish Church

The older inhabitants of Colne tell a story about the construction of their beautiful parish church, which sits in the centre of the town atop one of the seven hills upon which Colne, like Rome, is built.

The church was supposed to grace a site about half a mile out of town, at a spot known as Church Clough, but every night when the stonemasons left their labours, unseen hands moved their days work to its present situation. Nobody heard, or saw anyone carrying out this task, but as it was proving impossible to make any headway with the building, the founders decided to abandon their efforts at Church Clough and to build the church to where the spirits, hobgoblins, or whoever was moving the stones, had decreed it should stand.

Frankland's Mill

Frankland's mill is an old Victorian cotton-weaving shed situated in Walton Street, the top end of which, the locals call 'Coffin Lane'.

In July 2002, a man employed by Nelson Sheet Metal Engineering transferred, along with his press-brake machine, to a new location on the top floor of the building. It was then that he began to hear someone calling his name, but when he looked round to answer there was nobody there. The worker, being a very level-headed man, began to suspect that he was a victim of a practical joke, but none of his colleagues would admit to being the culprit. After a while he started to catch glimpses of a tall man wearing a shirt and waistcoat just behind him, but the image disappeared when the worker turned towards him.

The visitor appeared to be getting more confident and the press-brake operative could feel him looking over his shoulder as he programmed his machine. The worker told me that although the ghost's appearances made him feel apprehensive, he did not feel threatened by its seeming interest in modern technology. The ghost continued his visitations until 2004 when the firm moved to new premises in Padiham.

Greenfield Mill Cottages

In the 1970s Jean Peake went to visit her mother, Elizabeth Morville, at her old mill-workers' cottage on Greenfield Road. The road is now a cul-de-sac, but it was quite a busy thoroughfare before the construction of the new road between Barrowford and Colne. Jean told me that her mother was a down-to-earth woman who held no truck with ghosts and the like, but at a neighbour's insistence, had told her the following tale.

Elizabeth, or Lizzie as she was better known, had been cleaning a back bedroom at another one of the cottages, when she had sensed someone behind her: it was about eleven forty-five in the morning. As she turned to see who was there, she came face to face with the unattached head and shoulders of a young girl. Lizzie described her to Jean as 'a bonnie lass with a nice smile and dark curly hair'. Even though she did not feel threatened by the apparition, she was shocked and frightened and ran straight to her friend Kathleen's house to tell her what had happened.

Later that evening, the woman whose house she had been cleaning went to see Lizzie, and told her that the girl she described sounded like the woman who her young daughter had insisted kept coming into her bedroom at night.

Lizzie's friend, Kathleen Howarth, confirmed the story to me, saying that she believed Lizzie at the time, and still did because 'she was in a right state and wanted a cup of tea'.

Ghost at Hartley Hospital

When Eric Wilkinson took up a new post at Burnley General Hospital in the early 1970s, he moved into temporary accommodation in a top-floor flat at Colne's Hartley Hospital. During the six months that Eric, his wife Mavis, and their two young children, Rachel and Timothy, spent there, they became convinced that they were not alone.

Sometimes when the family were watching television in the sitting room, they would feel a blast of cold air as though someone had opened an outside door and, feeling that somebody was behind them, they would all turn round expecting to see a visitor. Their kitten, Ebony, also seemed unnerved at these times and would stand on the tips of her toes, her hair on end, back arched, and wide eyed with fear as she hissed and spat at some unseen presence.

Hartley Hospital, Colne - now apartments.

Eric recounted how he had often found himself holding open a door as he entered a room, mistakenly thinking that someone was behind him and Mavis described how she had woken panic stricken during the night to see the dark figure of a tall man, wearing a wide-brimmed hat and long cloak, at the foot of the bed. Not surprisingly, Mavis would pull the sheet over her head at these times, and wait until she sensed that the apparition had gone before emerging.

Eric and Mavis agreed that they had heard a 'swishing sound' as though somebody was dragging heavy laundry bags across the ceiling late at night, but on investigating they had found the roof space above their flat empty and unused.

After they moved to new living quarters, several colleagues told them that they were not the first people to experience strange happenings in the staff accommodation at the hospital and that no one had wanted to stay there for long.

Its biggest benefactor, Sir William P. Hartley, laid the foundation stone for Hartley hospital in 1921 and Christiana Hartley CBE, MA, JP officially opened the building in June 1924. After major conversion work, it is now a complex of luxurious retirement apartments.

The Tailor's cross. (courtesy of Lancashire County Library and Information Services)

The Tailor's Ghost

During the English Civil War, there were many skirmishes between the King's Cavaliers and Cromwell's Roundheads in and around the area. As time passed Cromwell's troops needed new clothes as theirs had fallen into disrepair. They rounded up all the local tailors and set them to work.

One of the captured tailors would not cooperate with these 'traitors' and refused to help their cause in any way, whereupon the soldiers shot him at a point about two hundred yards from Kirk Bridge, marking his grave with a stone on which they cut a pair of scissors as a warning to the others. The tailor sometimes appears in the area at midnight, groaning in pain and cursing his murderers.

EARBY

The Domesday Book refers to Earby as 'Eurebi in the manor of Thornton'.

The Peasey Family's Phantom

There was an unusual item on the agenda of Earby council's housing committee in December 1955. It concerned a rehousing request from the local chimney sweep, a Mr Peasey, and his family.

The family claimed that their house at number one Melrose Street was haunted, and they were too frightened to continue living there. They were sleeping in one small downstairs room, huddled together because of the terrifying events they had witnessed, and there being eleven Peaseys in all, this was clearly not a satisfactory arrangement.

The chimney sweep had written to the council stating that he had heard doors opening and shutting by themselves, followed by the sound of mysterious footsteps. He had also seen an apparition of a limbless darkened figure. His daughter Kathleen had witnessed two hooded figures in the bathroom, whilst his son, Bobby, claimed that a shadow had floated into the room and scratched him. Mrs Peasey told how her children woke screaming and terrified on many nights, and said she was thinking of contacting a spiritualist, as she could not cope much longer.

The members of the committee agreed that this situation could not continue, and that the family should be rehoused immediately.

EDISFORD

George

The Roefield Hotel, on the road out of Clitheroe at Edisford, closed its doors to thirsty locals and weary travellers many years ago. Whether the hotel's poltergeist stayed on to keep the new residents company, when it was transformed into a nursing home, is a matter for conjecture, as this venture too is shut down at the time of writing.

In March 1973, *The Clitheroe Advertiser and Times* ran a story telling how the entity, nicknamed 'George', had been getting up to mischief in an old wing of the building dating back to the early eighteenth century. A deep, beautifully crafted well, discovered during building work, suggests there may have been a house on the site long before the present structure. George's antics included opening and closing doors; turning appliances on and off; playing a non-existent piano and occasionally hurling things about.

Miss Doreen Burns, sister-in-law of Licensee Geoffrey Pilkington, claimed that a family member had seen George leaning on a beam in the attic. She described him as a youngish man, dressed casually in shirt and trousers.

Miss Burns went on to tell how she had encountered the spirit for the first time whilst she had been cleaning a bedroom in the old wing and the vacuum cleaner kept cutting out and restarting of its own accord. She added that on another occasion, she was collecting dirty linen from the same area when a banging door distracted her. She put the wicker laundry basket on the floor and went to shut the door. When she returned, there was a neat pile of wicker sticks on the carpet and a large hole in the basket.

Although George was generally good-natured, Miss Burns was again the victim in one of his more scary capers. She was climbing the cellar steps after hanging the washing to dry when something 'swished' past, frighteningly close to her head. She was amazed, and a little spooked, to see a pair of pyjamas land two steps in front of her.

Sometimes, there were other people on the receiving end of George's pranks. Members of staff reported dishes breaking in the kitchen and glasses smashing behind the bar when nobody was near them. They also claimed that objects had a habit of disappearing for a while before mysteriously turning up again. The Landlord told how he and his wife were relaxing in their sitting room before opening time one evening when they heard someone shout 'Hello', but on investigation, nobody else was in the building.

A customer witnessed George's best party trick when Miss Burns placed his change, a sixpenny piece, on the bar after serving him his usual tipple. The sixpence suddenly flew upwards, hit the ceiling, and landed on the other side of the room. The two startled onlookers were just recovering from the shock when, a few minutes later, George repeated his trick, and the coin flew threw the air once more this time landing back on the counter.

FENCE

The village of Fence takes its name from the enclosure in the area in which stags were contained following the demise of hunting in The Forest of Pendle. It has strong links with the Pendle Witches, who would have passed through the area whilst going about their daily business.

Ashlar House

Robert Nowell, the Justice of the Peace for Pendle Forest, questioned Old Demdike, Chattox, and Anne Redfearn at Ashlar House on 2 April 1612. Following his interrogation, the three women remained here, until they made the long journey to stand trial at Lancaster.

FOULRIDGE

There is some evidence that Foulridge, pronounced Foal ridge and lying about a mile and a half from Colne, was home to Bronze Age man. At the foot of nearby Noyna Crags, there is also an Iron Age wall.

Hobstones Farm

Hobstones farm dates back to the fifteenth century, although it is an eighteenth-century building that stands there today. The farm, now converted to several dwellings, lies to the east of Pendle hill, close to Lake Burwain, which takes its name from the old English word for 'burial place'. It is possible that the farm got its name from the hobgoblins that local myth says cavorted around this stony area.

Ashlar House, Fence, where witches were interrogated.

A ghostly Roundhead army strides the fields around Foulridge.

Hobstones Farm, where visiting spirits included a bloody monk. (courtesy of Lancashire Library and Information Services)

Although there are no records of actual hobgoblin sightings, several witnesses claim to have seen troops of armed Roundheads, striding across nearby fields armed with pikestaffs and swords. Sometimes officers accompany them on horseback. During the English civil war, the area was the location of skirmishes between Cromwell's troops and the King's cavaliers.

During the 1950s, another spectre made an appearance at Hobstones. A tenant farmer was apparently ensconced on the outside toilet just after daybreak, when a diminutive, ugly man dressed in a monk's habit confronted him. The monk had one hand severed just above his wrist, and blood was dripping freely from the stump. The farmer, paralysed by fear, watched for a few minutes as the apparition disintegrated and disappeared. The monk appeared to the farmer and his wife several times more, but no one saw the monk again after the couple moved away, unable to live with the ghostly presence.

In the 1970s, spooky things began to happen once again, during the conversion of the building into several apartments. It appears that this brought about an awakening of the infestation of poltergeist at Hobstones. Footsteps echoed around empty rooms, doors creaked open by themselves and objects moved mysteriously around the house. As the demonic activity increased, the building began to shake, windows smashed to the ground, and the walls made an awful ripping sound as if they were splitting apart.

Well known ghost hunter, Terence Whittaker, went to investigate and reported an incident in which a washing machine hurled itself across the kitchen taking with it a tray of eggs that was stored on its top. When the lady of the house went to clean up the mess, she discovered that all the white eggs were smashed, but the brown ones were still intact, forming the shape of a cross in the tray.

The owners consulted the rector of Colne, and he brought in an exorcist from the Fylde Coast who conducted a ceremony at Hobstones. The paranormal activity there now seems to have quietened down.

The New Inn

The New Inn stands on the old road between Foulridge and Skipton. It was originally a Friends Meeting House, and the remains of the Quaker churchyard still lie beneath the foundations of the pub's dining room. When renovations to this extension were taking place in the mid 1990s, builders unearthed remnants of many clay tobacco-pipes and assorted fragments of bones.

The inn has often been described as the most haunted pub in Pendle, being reputed to house the ghost of a cavalier, killed in a nearby battle, who knocks on the door of the master bedroom and a glowing cross which appears on the ceiling of the smallest bedroom. The present licensee, Barry Shepherd, has not witnessed either of these phenomena since taking over at The New Inn in April 1977, but eerie happenings at the pub have caused Barry, and his staff, to believe that the pub really does have a ghost or two.

Not long after Barry moved in, it was his habit to be first downstairs in the mornings so that he could switch on appliances and get the bar ready for the day's business. He frequently found dried flowers, from an arrangement in an old brass kettle that graced a window ledge, littering the floor of the taproom. There was no draught in the room, neither did the pub have a cat which could have knocked over the heavy kettle and Barry told me that it appeared that the flowers had been 'plucked' from their container before being scattered around. After several weeks of this, the landlord lost his patience at whatever was causing him extra work and yelled, 'Will you leave the bloody flowers alone? – I'm sick of this!'

His outburst seemed to stop this particular phenomenon, but other weird occurrences took its place: Both Barry and the cook, Danielle, described finding milk bottles arranged in the centre of the kitchen floor and one morning Danielle discovered several of them tilted to form a pyramid in the sink. She tried, along with other staff members, to recreate the tableau, but no one could get the bottles to balance.

The kitchen sink was also the site of what Barry calls his 'most unexplainable' experience. Whilst washing-up one day he lost a red stone from his ring and, assuming it had gone down the drain, he had it replaced. About nine months later Polly, a cleaner, found the stone on the very edge of the plughole after emptying the sink. The stone was smaller than the holes in the grid over the plughole, and many gallons of water had cascaded down the sink in the months since the stone disappeared.

Another cleaner, Helen, refused to enter the Gents' toilets for several weeks, after seeing a ghostly figure watching at a high internal window as she mopped the floor, and some of the pub's older regular customers will not use one of the cubicles in the ladies toilet as they always feel there is someone else in there with them.

The New Inn,
Foulridge - reputed to
be the most haunted
pub in Pendle.

The only time Barry feels that he has actually 'seen' a ghost was when he was tidying up after closing time one evening and he saw a tall silhouette float across the bar towards the ladies toilet, where it disappeared through the door. Despite having 'goose bumps as big as golf balls' he went to investigate but found he was totally alone, as he had thought.

The spooky incidents at The New Inn seem to escalate and then stop for a while. Eventually though objects will start to move once again from wherever they were left, or the music system will turn on by itself, as though the ghost is reminding the mere mortals at the pub that it is still with them.

GARGRAVE

The Gargrave Witch

Anne Greene lived at Gargrave in the seventeenth century. She made a meagre living by selling potions, lotions, and charms to her deeply superstitious neighbours.

One of these neighbours, John Tatterson, went to consult her with earache, but was not satisfied with the black wool that Anne advised him to place in his ear as a remedy. Eager not to loose her payment, Anne took off her garter and hit Tatterson's ear with it three times. She then plucked some hair from the back of his neck, and sent him on his way.

Her patient's earache got worse and he returned, determined that she should cure his pain. Anne again struck his ear three times with her garter, this time chanting a spell as she did so. Foul smelling matter then began to ooze from the ear, and as it drained away, Tatterson's pain went with it. The story spread, and Anne's reputation grew until the country people around Gargrave believed her to have supernatural powers.

A woman called Margaret Wade had a daughter, Elizabeth, who became ill. It was rumoured that Anne Greene had caused the child's sickness and other stories of her supposed ill doings began to emerge. When Wade told how she had seen Anne, in the form of a large two-legged dog, in her daughter's bedroom the local magistrate sent her to York to stand trial for witchcraft.

GISBURN

Gisburn's parish church has Norman windows with stained glass dating back to the fourteenth century. Guy of Gisburn, from the Robin Hood legend, supposedly came from this farming town.

The Gisburn Witch

Although Jennet Preston was at the notorious Good Friday feast at Malkin Tower, she did not stand trial along with the Pendle witches because she lived in Gisburn, which was then part of Yorkshire.

Jennet Preston was a poor country woman from Westby, between Gisburn and Blacko. She was a frequent, and welcome, visitor to the home of the Lister family, who would give her food and drink. The friendship, however, seemed to deteriorate after the death of Thomas Lister, and his son, also called Thomas, blamed Jennet for any illness or ill luck that befell his family. His animosity culminated in his implicating her in the death of a child, for which she faced trial, and cleared her name, at York in 1612.

A Norman window at the parish church in Gisburn, the home of executed witch, Jennet Preston.

Soon after her release from prison, she was amongst those found consorting with the Pendle witches at Malkin Tower and the justices had her hauled back to York to face a charge brought against her by Thomas Lister's father-in-law. The revengeful man, and his family, accused Jennet of killing Thomas Lister senior, by witchcraft, five years earlier.

One witness, Anne Robinson, testified that Lister had cried out an accusation against Jennet on his deathbed, and that Jennet had come to lay him out when he died. She told the court that when the woman had touched Lister's corpse it had begun to bleed profusely. According to a superstition of the time, this would only happen when a murderer touched a victim's body, so this was offered as proof of Jennet's guilt. Further evidence, including that of James Device, who claimed he had seen her change herself into a white foal, led to a guilty verdict and Jennet Preston went to the gallows at York, two weeks before the Lancaster trial of her cronies began.

The Ribblesdale Arms

This hotel, which dates back to 1635, ended its life as a public house at the beginning of the twenty-first century. Whilst it was still in use as a watering hole by locals and visitors alike, it reputedly harboured the ghost of a young girl who was expecting a baby to one of the past Lord Ribblesdales. Both staff and guests at the old coaching house spotted her on several occasions, in and around room eighteen.

The Ghost at Stirk House

After the dismantling of Sawley Abbey during Henry VIII's dissolution of the monasteries, the builders used some of the stone to renovate and extend Stirk House.

The Ribblesdale Arms, now a private residence.

Sawley Abbey. Stones from here were used in renovations at Stirk House.

The house was a private dwelling owned by the Lister family and later the Hartleys of Colne, and did not function as licensed premises until 1935. Since then, many strange occurrences have taken place: Ghostly shadows in rooms and corridors, the sound of shattering glass – but no shards, and a monk who appears to be looking out from one of the mullioned windows that came from Sawley Abbey. A guest at the Hotel in 2005 told how she had woken up to find a ghostly face peering into hers, causing her to scream and jump out of bed in fright.

Opinion is split as to who is responsible for the haunting. One possibility is that it is the spirit of a vicar from Skipton, waylaid and murdered on his journey between Sawley and Gisburn. Another theory is that it is the ghost of an abbot, Father William Trafford, whose hanging Henry VIII, ordered because of his resistance to the dissolution of the monasteries. A third candidate is millionaire Alec Ormerod, who owned the house in the early twentieth century. The financier, who committed suicide following the London stock market crash, had his ashes scattered on the old tennis courts, where the hotel ballroom now stands.

GOOSNARGH

Chingle Hall

Chingle Hall is, reputedly, the most haunted house in England. The hall, built by Adam de Singleton in 1260 and originally called Singleton Hall, may be the oldest inhabited, brick-built house in the country. Some of its wooden beams bear ancient symbols, and are probably salvage pieces from the remains of a Viking longboat, which sank in the River Ribble.

The Martyr's Ghost

The Singletons were devout Roman Catholics and during the Reformation, they built several priest holes, two of which are hidden in the family chapel. The last English Roman Catholic martyr, John Wall, was born at Chingle in 1612 after his family, relations of the Singletons, moved there in the late sixteenth century. A company of the King's men arrested him whilst he was conducting a mass at the hall and he faced execution for heresy at Worcester in 1679. His loyal followers took his severed head around the country; some say they got as far as France, before they brought it back, to bury it in a cellar at Chingle.

Many people have reported seeing the martyr's ghost, dressed in a monk's habit, roaming through the Hall and its grounds.

Eleanor's Room

Visitors to Eleanor's room generally tell of a feeling of overwhelming sadness encompassing them. One legend of the hall says that murder of twenty-year-old Eleanor Singleton took place in her bedroom, after she had been a prisoner there for more than twelve years.

The Floating Man

There have been many sightings of a man with shoulder-length hair walking past a window in the priest's room. This has caused a few surprises, as the window is twelve feet from the ground.

Monks

Hooded monks seem to be a common apparition seen at Chingle both in the Hall itself and in its gardens. A few years ago, restorers found an old wooden cross under thick plaster in the chapel, and there have been sightings of monks seen kneeling before the same chapel wall as if in prayer.

A phantom hand sometimes shows itself as though moving bricks in the priest's room and a drawbridge, replaced several centuries ago by a solid one, still creaks and clatters open from time to time.

GRINDLETON

Some of the cottages in and around Grindleton date from pre-industrial times when their inhabitants would weave cloth on handlooms.

The Witch's Familiar

The villages around Pendle Hill had 'witches' other than those who were hanged at Lancaster in 1612. Woven into the folklore of Grindleton, near Clitheroe, is the story of a local witch who had the power to change her shape.

One day, a weaver went into his hand-weaving shed and saw a strange cat crawling around the floor in a very un-cat-like manner. He felt disconcerted by the animal's behaviour and when the cat refused to respond to his attempts to shoo it away, the weaver caught it and hung it by the neck until it died.

Later the same day, the Grindleton 'witch', who had seemed well the previous day, was found dead in her bed. The villagers connected the two incidents and the weaver received their gratitude for ridding them of the old hag.

The Boggarts of West Clough Wood

In the early 1800s, farmers around Chipping and Waddington Fell frequently reported sightings of boggarts. These creatures were supposedly larger than rabbits or hares, and moved quickly over the moorland.

In 1820, a church verger paused to light his pipe whilst walking through West Clough Wood. He heard a rustling sound and found himself surrounded by imp-like figures who seemed as surprised to see him, as he was to see them. After this incident, people went to the woods to see the boggarts for themselves, and not many were disappointed.

Sometimes, however, the boggarts showed their dark side, and the villagers accused them of stampeding cattle and throwing stones at local farmhouses.

HAPTON

Hapton, a small village near Padiham, was one of the first places to have electric streetlights. On the nearby moors, some earthworks and a few scattered pieces of masonry are all that remain of a fourteenth-century castle, whilst ruins that are rather more substantial still stand on the site of an old Towneley family hunting lodge.

Canal-side Hauntings

The Bridge House Inn stands on the banks of the Leeds-Liverpool canal in the village of Hapton. In the days when the canals were the transport backbone of the region, bargees used to rest their horses in the stables at the side of the inn when they moored up for the night. This stable is now the pub's beer cellar and adjoins, but does not connect to, another smaller cellar at the back of the inn. This second cellar has steps leading down to it from the canal towpath and houses a stone slab, upon which in days gone by, any bodies pulled from the canal's murky waters would be stored until burial.

One such victim was a young servant girl called Alice who threw herself from a nearby bridge and drowned after suffering a broken romance, and several past Licencees have claimed to be aware of her ghost. Sometimes Alice mounts the steps of the mortuary cellar and disappears into an old pantry, whilst at other times she hovers around the fireplace in the oldest part of the building.

Dawn Millar, who took over the Bridge House Inn in early 2006, told me that she had experienced several spooky happenings since moving in. She often senses a dog or cat around her feet when serving behind the bar and has sometimes moved to let the animal pass, thinking it to be her own dog, only to find she is stepping around thin air. Her dog Nappa, however, seems to have his own ghostly experiences when he will run towards the old fireplace clearly agitated, and barking at nothing. Dawn also described how she sensed someone behind her early one morning when she was collecting ashtrays. Glancing over her shoulder, she saw a small dark shadow move towards the same fireplace, but could find no explanation for it.

Top: Serving girl Alice is thought to have jumped from this canal bridge at Hapton.

Above: The stone slab in the cellar of the Bridge House Inn which was used for storing bodies awaiting burial.

Left: Old steps leading from the canal path to the cellar of the Bridge House inn.

Another spirit is reputed to haunt the old stable. This one is a more mature woman, dressed in rough clothing, who may have had some connection to stable work.

Dawn's husband, Darren, was initially quite sceptical about the ghosts, but changed his mind following an eerie experience of his own. Dawn had been discussing their spectral visitors with some customers and Darren had dismissed the possibility of any hauntings saying that there must be logical explanations for the phenomena. As he expressed his opinion, he approached the jukebox intending to play something to lighten the mood. As he rested his hands on the casing, the machine began to shake and vibrate vigorously, only stopping when Darren removed his hands. The jukebox had never done this before, nor has it repeated its performance since.

HIGHAM

The ancient village of Higham has strong connections with the Pendle witches, especially Chattox.

The Four Alls
The sign decorating the front of the Four Alls Inn depicts a worker – 'I pay for all'; a soldier, 'I fight for all'; a judge, 'I govern all' and a church minister, 'I pray for all'.

Thomas Grimshaw built the house in 1792, as a present for his future wife Grace Gibson and a worn inscription above the door shows their entwined initials.

David and Pauline Holden have been tenants at the pub since 2000, and Pauline in particular has had some strange experiences since moving in. The poolroom seems to be the focus of ghostly attention, with regulars seeing the phantom of an elderly gentleman sitting in the corner of the bar. Although Pauline has not seen this old customer herself, she told me that she was Hoovering the pub one day when she felt some one push past her at the doorway. Thinking it was David, she turned round to speak to him, but the poolroom was empty. Pauline said she felt as though her hair was standing on end and that she knew that some one, or something, had definitely passed her.

The landlady felt that this ghostly visitor was a man, but she has also seen the figure of a young girl walking through the bar area and disappearing through a wall near to the toilet doors. The men's toilet in the pub, used to form part of the building that was once a butcher and slaughter-man's shop. It has a spring-loaded door, which makes a very distinctive sound when it closes, and it needs 'a good shove' to open it. David and Pauline have heard this door squeaking open, when they have been alone in their flat above the pub with the outside doors locked and barred.

The upstairs rooms at the Four Alls were reputedly a courtroom at some stage in the building's history, but the couple have never noticed anything untoward up there. The cellar, however, is another matter, being exceptionally cold at times and so creepy that the family dog refuses to go into it. According to some villagers, a tunnel may have once led from the cellar to the Methodist chapel graveyard across the road, and bodies awaiting burial were stored there.

HIGHERFORD

The Dicky Nook ghost
Dicky Nook barn used to stand at the junction of Gisburn Road and Barnoldswick Road in the area of Higherford known as Canaan in Victorian times. It took its name from a man called Dicky Stansfield, a one–time occupant of an attached cottage. It was demolished in 1924. Jesse Blakey's *The Annals of Barrowford* mentions the following chilling tale.

The Four Alls Inn, Higham.

Pub sign at the Four Alls Inn.

The Methodist graveyard, which may once have been reached by a tunnel from the cellar of the Four Alls.

Left: Dicky Nook, as it looked before 1924.

In the early nineteenth century, a young man named William Bracewell was heading towards Higherford on his way home from band practice. When he got close to Dicky Nook he encountered a small, wizened old man dressed in knee breeches and buckled shoes. He had an apron tucked into the side of his belt and was enveloped in a strange glow.

A terrified William took to his heels, and ran the rest of the way home. When he had recovered his breath he told his mother what he had seen, and she replied that it sounded like little Holt, a local cobbler who had died a few years earlier. It later transpired that a neighbour, James Clegg, had also seen the apparition, and a church meeting was convened to discuss the matter. Jessie Blakely reports that Clegg was told to quote the Holy Trinity if he saw the ghost again.

A while later, on a second sighting of little Holt, he carried out churchmen's instructions and challenged the cobbler saying 'In the name of the Father, and of the Son, and of the Holy Ghost, what wantest thou?' whereupon the Dicky Nook ghost melted into the night and was never seen again.

HURST GREEN

The Devil's Bridge

Richard Shireburn built the old packhorse bridge spanning the River Hodder at Hurst green in 1562 to replace a much earlier wooden one. Some people call it 'Cromwell's Bridge' due to their belief that the bridge lost its sides when Oliver Cromwell ordered their removal to enable his supply wagons to cross the river, as he travelled from Skipton to intercept the Royalist troops at Preston in 1648.

The structure, also known locally as 'The Devil's Bridge' has had an evil reputation for many years. It is supposed to be the site of the rape and murder of an innocent milkmaid and there have been reports of the unfortunate girl's ghost returning to haunt the bridge, wailing and rocking her ravaged body.

Another local legend, which is possibly the reason for the bridge's name, has it that anyone crossing it on All Hallow's Eve is likely to meet the Devil, and the following tale illustrates the foolishness of going against this advice.

Humphrey Dobson was born in Lancaster in 1750 and by the time he was twenty-four he was an official on the estate of Lord Lowther. By all accounts, he was a cruel and arrogant man who took laudanum and indulged in alcohol to excess. On the evening of Halloween 1774, Dobson was in a furious temper. He had received a warning from Lord Lowther that he would be dismissed if his drunken foul-mouthed behaviour did not improve, and he suspected that a

The Devil's Bridge at Hurst Green.

man called Calvert had informed on him. He worked himself up into such a rage that his temper snapped and he jumped onto his horse and set off to find his betrayer. Calvert was staying at the Bayley Arms at Hurst Green.

In an effort to deter him, Dobson's wife Florence recounted the legend of the Devil's Bridge, which he would have to cross to get there, but he was beyond reason and set off at a gallop through the frosty moonless night. He spent the evening drinking ale and sipping his laudanum at the pub. Calvert, however, did not appear so after leaving word that he would return to extract his revenge on another night he set off on the long ride home. As Dobson approached the Devil's Bridge this time, his horse refused to cross, and fuelled by drink and drugs he whipped it into a frenzy until it continued on its way. As the frightened horse pounded over the span, Dobson heard a blood-curdling scream and felt the iron grip of icy hands close around his waist. He turned to look at his uninvited pillion passenger and saw a grinning, eyeless skull shining white against the backdrop of the night sky. He screamed until his throat bled, pulling at the gripping arms to release their hold, but saw that they too were just bare bones. Eventually his mount threw him, knocking him unconscious in the process. When he woke, it was daylight and he managed to stagger home where he collapsed on the doorstep.

When Florence found him lying there, she could hardly believe what she saw: Her husband's hair had turned white, whilst deep lines of horror criss-crossed his face. Dobson did not speak for five years, neither did he ever leave the grounds of his house again for fear of meeting the Devil, whom the locals claim still lurks under the bridge waiting for another victim.

The Highwayman

Ned King was a notorious eighteenth-century highwayman who, dressed in a fashionable red coat and white frilled shirt with matching breeches, accosted travellers in the lanes around Longridge and Clitheroe.

Above left: Pub sign at The Punchbowl inn, depicting the highwayman Ned King.

Above right: The lane where Ned King was taken to be hanged.

He was in league with the landlord of the Punchbowl inn, an old coaching house dating back to 1793. The dastardly innkeeper would inform Ned when wealthy patrons called in for refreshments and a change of horses so that Ned could wait in his favourite hidden spot on the road and waylay them as they recommenced their journey.

Eventually the king's men captured Ned as he hid in the barn of the Punchbowl inn, and took him away and hanged the highwayman without trial in nearby Gallows Lane.

The ghost of Ned King has haunted the pub for over two centuries, and despite a local priest performing an exorcism there in 1942, he continues to make his presence felt by moaning from the barn (now a dining room) and banging along corridors late at night.

On several occasions, when the ghost has been having an active period, bottles have fallen from shelves and shattered without any obvious reason for doing so.

LANESHAWBRIDGE

Laneshawbridge stands at the crossroads of what used to be several turnpike roads, one of which, built in the mid-eighteenth century, still winds its way past the ancient and very haunted hamlet of Wycoller, across open moorland to the Brontës' hometown, Haworth.

Hannah Corbridge

A marginal note in Colne Parish Register of Baptisms and Burials 1774-1779 (transcribed by Gladys Whittaker) reads:

Corbridge, Hannah 29.7.1789 – On the 29th of this month was interred at New Church in Pendle, the body of Hannah Corbridge, of this Chapelry. Concerning whom the following narrative deserves to be recorded. She went off on Sunday forenoon the 19th inst from her father's house at Narrs, with her lover Christopher Hartley, of Barnside a youth of 19 years of age, by whom she was big with child. She was never seen afterwards, till the next Sunday forenoon, when she was found, near home, dead in a ditch, being poisoned, and having her throat cut so deep that her head only hung by two teguments behind.

On the next Sunday forenoon 2nd August the murderer was brought back to Colne, having been
apprehended at Flookborough; was found guilty by the coroners Inquest, committed to Lancaster, convicted
and executed August 28th.

Although there is no mention of how Christopher Hartley poisoned his young girlfriend in this account, legend has it that he gave her a slice of poisoned parkin, a local type of gingerbread, as they rested in the grass during a regular Sunday morning stroll. The spot was not far from Hartley's home at Barnside Hall so after finishing off his grisly morning's work by cutting Hannah's throat, he dragged her body home and hid it in an old chest for a while. When Hannah's family reported her missing from her home at Knarrs End, the constables paid the Hartleys a visit, but found nothing untoward. This must have frightened the young killer, as he then moved the corpse to a field known as 'Northings' which lay about a quarter of a mile from Barnside Hall.

J. Carr in his *Annals and Stories of Colne and Neighbourhood* (1878) tells of the superstition that surrounded the discovery of Hannah's body after a relative of the girl consulted a wise man at Todmorden. The Oracle told him where to look but warned him not to approach the spot himself or he would be 'haunted forever'. The relative took this advice and supervised the search from a hillside vantage point, but he must have got too close because soon after Hannah's body was found and her murderer hanged by his neck her ghost was regularly seen wandering the neighbourhood at midnight.

A local farmer called in a Catholic priest to lay her spirit to rest, and he held a ceremony, in which the priest bargained with Hannah's ghost not to reappear whilst the candle that was burning in the room had burnt out. When the spirit agreed, and took her leave, the cunning priest instantly swallowed the candle stub to prevent the possibility of it ever burning away. This seemed to have the required effect as Hannah's ghost became less troublesome afterwards.

The story, however, does not end there because years later, following the demolition of Barnside Hall, many of its stones were carried to Laneshawbridge and used in buildings and bridges in the village. There then began to be reports of some of these stones oozing blood, especially the one that forms part of the parapet of the hump back bridge in the centre of Laneshawbridge. Reports of people witnessing this phenomenon still crop up in local newspapers from time to time, particularly during wet weather.

Laneshawbridge. There have been reports of blood oozing from the stonework.

Whilst the rationale is that this 'oozing blood' is probably caused by a chemical reaction within the stone during rainfall, there are still some who believe it is the blood of Hannah Corbridge: absorbed from her lifeless body, or from the hands of her killer, Christopher Hartley, as he used the stones to wipe her blood from his hands.

The Lady in Brown

The Colne Times newspaper reported that an un-named man had seen a spectral figure near to the Hargreaves Arms in November 1994.

The ghost, a woman dressed in a long brown cape and wearing stout boots, came out from a wall by the pub car park, crossed the road, and merged into some trees where she vanished. The newspaper article quoted the startled motorist as saying, 'Whatever it was, it was not a human being in the natural sense. I don't know what it was, but it was real'.

Because of the Hargreaves Arms' position on the outskirts of Laneshawbridge, this sighting led to speculation that the spirit of Hannah Corbridge still wandered the area.

Reedymoor Farmhouse

Reedymoor farm lies across from Hobstones, on the other side of Lake Burwain. It is about six years newer than Hobstones and it is possible that the 'hob' (from hobgoblins) stones used in both constructions were from the same local quarry.

It was a working farm up until 1965, and retains many of its original features, including heavy doors with latches that need lifting and lowering again in order to open them. After many years of disuse, the old farmhouse became a guesthouse and the new owners and their paying guests began to have some spooky experiences.

They would hear footsteps in empty rooms and find doors they had previously closed with the latch standing wide open. Guests reported at breakfast time that their doors rattled and shook during the night, as though someone or something was trying to get into their rooms. The owners dog refused to go upstairs on his own, and family members felt 'a presence' when they were alone in the house. No-one ever saw the ghost, who they named 'George', and as the children grew up and left home, he became a less frequent visitor.

The Standing Stones Stagecoach

A one-time resident of Standing Stone Farm claimed that the pounding of horses' hooves and creaking of wheels outside the former coaching inn had woken her one night. Someone then banged on the door and demanded that she let them in, but when the woman looked out of the window to see what the commotion was, there was no one there, nor was there any sign of a vehicle, horse-drawn or otherwise.

LONGRIDGE

It is thought by some that the town of Longridge got its name from a comment that Oliver Cromwell made when he passed by the fell on his way to the battle of Preston. From the top of Longridge fell, it is possible to see as far as the Welsh mountains and the Isle of Man when conditions are favourable.

The Longridge Witch

In the early part of the seventeenth century, a severe drought affected the Ribble Valley. The hedges withered and the fields turned to dust, causing the cattle to become thin, weak with hunger, and unable to give milk. Consequently the people of the area were also hungry, thirsty, and in need of nourishment.

One farmer, however, had a large well-fattened dun cow that was rumoured to be fed by the fairies every night. The grateful farmer wanted to help the villagers, so he allowed them to milk his beast and share the milk amongst themselves. The village folk appreciated this act of kindness, and were fair in taking only what they needed, so that all could benefit.

A spiteful and malicious old hag, who was known as 'The Longridge Witch' came to hear of this remarkable cow and was outraged that the fairies were interfering on her domain. She rose early one morning and went in search of the dun cow, which she began to milk before the villagers had time to do the job. When they saw the witch taking their milk they watched at a distance, waiting for her to finish.

The witch carried on milking for hours, cackling that she would not stop until her can was full. Eventually the animal collapsed and died of exhaustion and as the villagers ran to its aid, they

Reedymoor Farmhouse. (courtesy of Lancashire Library and Information Services)

saw that the witch had been milking her into a sieve, and the ground had absorbed the liquid.

After carving the best meat from his cow, the farmer gave the carcass to the villagers, helping them to survive until the drought was over. They mounted one of the beast's ribs over the door of a cottage, now known as 'Old Rib House' to commemorate the event.

Many years later, pranksters pried the rib loose and threw it into the nearby river, but so much bad luck plagued them that they retrieved the relic and replaced it in its rightful position.

The Written Stone Boggart

Written Stone Farm stands along an old Roman road in Dilworth, which is about two miles from Longridge. It takes its name from an old weatherworn stone that lies nearby. The stone measures nine feet in length, is two feet wide, one foot in thickness, and has a deeply-carved inscription, which reads:

RAVFFE RADCLIFFE LAID THIS STONE TO LYE FOR EVER AD 1655

Some think that this stone marks the spot where a murderous boggart was imprisoned. This evil spirit made a habit of terrorising travellers along the lonely lane by punching and scratching them as they passed. His ungodly howls and screeches echoed around the lanes until Ravffe Radcliffe captured and entombed him under the stone. Others are of the opinion that the monolith was merely laid by Radcliffe to commemorate some important family event. Whatever the reason for the stone's existence a former occupant of the farm made a mistake in not allowing it 'to lye for ever'!

The legend is that this farmer decided it would be a good stone to use in his dairy, and its cold surface would be ideal for making butter. As soon as the farmhands installed it as such, pots, pans, jugs, and anything else they put on its surface would fall over, spilling their contents and rolling and rattling about together. It seemed that the spirit, or boggart, that had lain under the stone was unhappy with its new position.

This continued for quite some time until the farmer, exhausted by lack of sleep, returned the stone to its previous site. From thenceforward, order returned to Written Stone Farm, and the farmer and his wife, slept peacefully in their bed once more.

The Headless Hag

Another malicious boggart is associated with the lanes around Longridge, although some claim that the Written Stone boggart and the Headless Woman are the same spirit under different guises. This apparition would appear as an old woman walking slowly down the lane carrying a basket under her arm. She wore an old-fashioned fringed shawl and a large bonnet, pulled well down. She would walk companionably alongside other travellers, her head bowed as though listening carefully to their polite conversation and then she would suddenly turn towards them to reveal that she was headless. As her terrified victims took this in, she would pull the cloth from her basket, whereupon her head would leap from it, and howling and snapping like a vicious dog, it would chase them for miles.

MELLOR

The Miserly Ghost of Sykes Lumb Farm

At the time of the Wars of the Roses, Farmer Sykes and his wife had accumulated a fortune, due to their meanness and hoarding. They had no children to inherit their riches, or to run Sykes Lumb Farm when they were gone, but they still set great store by their earthly possessions. The stingy couple were worried that marauding bands from the opposing armies fighting nearby would learn of their wealth, so they decided to stash the money in earthenware jars and bury these in the orchard.

After many years the farmer died, followed some time later by his wife, whose death was so sudden that she did not have time to tell anyone where she had hidden the money. Her relatives scoured the farm, but without luck and Sykes Lumb then passed into stranger's hands.

People may have forgotten the story of the buried treasure, if it was not for the regular return of the farmer's wife's ghost. Locals, from nearby Samlesbury, reported seeing her apparition over many generations and almost all described her as having a wrinkled face, a striped petticoat, and leaning on an old crooked stick.

Eventually, one tenant of the farm, made brave through drink, challenged her to reveal the whereabouts of the treasure trove. The miserly ghost glided slowly and silently towards the orchard, where she pointed to the roots of an ancient gnarled apple tree. The farmer took his spade and dug into the ground, whilst Old Sykes' wife watched. When he had unearthed the last jar, she smiled at him, and her spectre slowly disintegrated – and was never seen again.

The Sykes Lumb Farm Boggart

There is also a legend of a boggart, or poltergeist at Sykes Lumb Farm, although it is unclear at what period in the farm's history this took place.

The boggart was generally quite pleasant and helpful, but if he felt that he was not receiving due respect from the inhabitants he became angry and revengeful. When roused he would hurl pots and pans around the kitchen, tamper with farm machinery to cause accidents, and let the animals out of their enclosures. Sometimes he took pleasure in pulling the cover off the beds, ensuring that no one had a good night's sleep. His favourite perch was a beam in the barn from where he could watch, and gloat over, the consequences of his mischief.

Sykes Lumb, like many other farms and cottages in the area, no longer exists. There is now an airfield and aero-engineering plant covering the site.

MITTON

The village of Mitton takes its name from its position as the 'mid-town' between the River Ribble and the River Hodder.

The Three Fishes Inn

The three fish pendant of Abbot Paslew, whose ghost haunts nearby Whalley Abbey, appears carved into the stonework above the door of the Three Fishes Inn. The Inn was a notorious hiding place of criminals and highwaymen during the late sixteenth and early seventeenth centuries and its cellars probably housed several of the Pendle Witches before they went to their deaths at Lancaster in 1612.

NELSON

Before adopting the name of Nelson in honour of the famous admiral's achievements, the community that once existed where the textile and engineering town now stands had the name of Marsden.

Little Emily

When Jayne Spears and Sara Buckle were house hunting in early 2005, they found themselves strongly attracted to a property in Eagle Street Nelson. The friends told me that although they had viewed more up-to-date houses they felt comfortable as soon as they walked through the door of this terraced cottage and felt almost compelled to move in.

From their first day in Eagle Street, Sara sensed a female 'presence' there and the two cats of the household seemed 'spooked' at times, arching their backs and staring fixedly at a spot near the kitchen doorway.

Jayne's brother, Anthony Spears, has built up something of a reputation for his sensitivity in detecting spirits and, along with Jayne and Sarah, he is an active member of The Ghost Club. When he first visited them in their new home, they had not told him about their suspected ghost, but shortly after his arrival, he saw a little girl upstairs who was jumping excitedly up and down. The child, aged about six or seven, was wearing a brown coat, white petticoat and black shoes and stockings. She told him that her name was Emily.

Since showing herself to Anthony, Emily appears to have got used to Jayne and Sara. They often hear her childish giggles and sense her excitement, especially when they are carrying out home improvements or operating their computers. She is most active after ten-o-clock at night, when the friends often hear her walking up and down the staircase.

They claim that Emily also has a mischievous side to her nature, hiding articles such as the television remote before returning them to their original, obvious, positions a few days later. Jayne's mother was the victim of a similar prank when her make-up case disappeared during a recent visit, only to reappear on the dressing table where she had left it, after two days. Anthony's computer also restarted mysteriously when he turned it off after playing music.

Sara described one occasion when they had gone out for the day, leaving a tea light on a piece of paper in the back bedroom where they feel Emily once slept. Before they left, they drew a

Above: 'Little Emily'. (Anthony Spears)

Top left and left: Photographs of 'orbs' taken by Jayne Spears and Sara Buckle.

circle around the tea light and asked the child's spirit to move it. They claim that when they came home, the light had moved about an inch out of the circle.

Although Jayne and Sara are comfortable with Emily, they have felt other less friendly spirits around the house. Sara has seen a tall black shape materialise in the corner of her bedroom, and Jayne was in the kitchen when she heard someone breathing behind her. As she turned around to investigate, the oven door banged shut and she felt very uneasy. Jayne is convinced that this was a visit from a spirit other than Emily.

The friends have taken several photographs of what they identify as 'orbs', and say that these only show up on film when they, and their cats, can feel a presence. The orbs often manifest themselves around the kitchen doorway and a sharp drop in temperature sometimes accompanies them. Jane and Sara believe that this area of the house may be a 'portal' through which visitors from the spirit world come and go.

The Blind Spectre
In the index boxes at Nelson library there is a drawer marked 'Local History Snippets'. One of them contains the report of a child seeing the pale ghost of an old lady at her home in Townhouse Road,

during the 1960s. The child told of the woman holding out her hands in front of her, as if to feel her way, and the parents recognised the description of the spectre as fitting the child's great - grandmother who had been blind when she had died at the age of ninety-two.

Children's Laughter

Michelle and David Brooks have lived in their terraced house in Garrick Street since 1982. When they moved in, Ann, their eldest daughter was five years old and they often heard tiny footsteps running across the upstairs floor whilst they watched television late in the evenings. One of them would go to put Ann back in her bed, only to find her already tucked-up and sleeping soundly.

Michelle told me how she often felt the presence of children, particularly at the top of the stairs, and that several times she had heard a girl's voice calling 'Mummy' when she was alone in the house. When she told David about her experiences, he replied that he had similar ones when he was sleeping during the daytime after working night shift. On these occasions, he had woken when the bedroom door flew open and had heard the sound of children laughing and running away, as though playing a trick.

When Michelle became pregnant with their second daughter, Victoria, in 1987, the ghostly children seemed to have left the house and all was quiet for a while, but two days after the couple brought their new baby home they were back. Michelle and David also mistakenly thought that the ghostly activity would stop when they completely gutted and rebuilt the interior of their home in 1990, but the first night that they returned to their re-furbished house, they heard the little footsteps once more.

The playful spirits still visit Garrick Street, but seem to go quiet if something sad is happening in the family. At times like this, Michelle and David are glad when they hear the children's laughter again, as it usually means that things are looking brighter for them once more.

Witch's Breath

Even witches must die and a thread of folklore has it that a witch may pass on her familiar, and therefore her magic powers, through her dying breath.

As late as the nineteenth century, it was still a common belief in Pendle that some women regularly practised the art of witchcraft. One of these suspected witches was an ancient crone called Peggy, who lived in a hovel at Marsden (now Nelson). She struck such fear into her superstitious neighbours that, although she had no income, she never went hungry. If the old woman did not get food from one or the other of them, she would curse and threaten until they met her demands. If illness or bad luck then struck, they would attribute it to her powers, so were reluctant to cross her.

When Peggy realised that she was on her deathbed, she called for her brother's granddaughter to visit her as a matter of urgency. When the frightened girl arrived, Peggy motioned for her to kneel by her bed whilst she chanted a spell over her. This done, she embraced her, breathing her last breath into the child's mouth.

The story does not continue further, or explain whether the girl went on to emulate her great aunt, nor are there any further legends linked to the episode.

NEWBRIDGE

The Peevish Poltergeist

In the late 1990s, a young couple bought their first home in Nora Street, Newbridge and moved in with their baby daughter. On their first night, they lay awake listening to what sounded like

Newbridge. (courtesy of Lancashire Library and Information Services)

footsteps crossing and re-crossing the floor of the upstairs rooms. They put this phenomenon down to the age of the house and got used to it recurring from time to time.

Over the next few years, the footsteps increased and other odd things began to happen. A visitor thanked the woman of the house for replacing the cover on her bed, but no one had done so, the couple heard coat hangers in the wardrobe rattling and sliding from side to side and the woman sensed a small male figure standing at the top of the staircase several times.

When the couple's daughter was four years old, she started to wake in the night, screaming for her mummy and saying there was a man in her room. She also said her dummy (pacifier) was flying across the room and that red and green lights were coming through the wall above her head then moving swiftly up and down her bed. The couple made as little fuss as possible about the child's night terrors, hoping she would outgrow them, but one night the mother went into soothe the screaming child and found her wide-eyed and terrified in the corner of her bed. As the mother crossed the room to reach her, a box containing old jewellery, which the girl used for dressing-up games, flew violently off a chest of drawers and crashed to the floor at the woman's feet. The woman remembers that the room felt very cold.

The next day the little girl asked if the man had gone and added 'You know... the one you walked through at the door.'

The couple asked their local vicar to come and bless their house, which he did. After he had left, the child told her mother that the lights had 'whooshed' through the window, and the family were then left in peace.

NEWCHURCH-IN-PENDLE

Newchurch-In-Pendle nestles next to its neighbour, Barley, at the foot of Pendle Hill. It was called Goldshaw before 1529, when the parishioners built a church on the site of a thirteenth-century chapel of ease. The church was consecrated to St Mary in 1544, but was generally referred to as 'the new church' thus eventually giving the village the same name.

Above: A Nutter family grave in the churchyard at Newchurch, known as 'The witch's grave'. (Peto Veritum)

Left: 'The Eye of God' on the tower of St Mary's church, Newchurch-in-Pendle.

The 'Eye of God'

The present church of St Mary was finished in 1740, and the only remaining structure of the sixteenth-century building is the tower. The tower bears a large grey/blue eye sculpted into its west face, which represents the all-seeing eye of God. This was supposed to protect the villagers from evil, and deter the witches of Pendle Forest from stealing bones from the graveyard to use in their spells.

The Witch's Grave

To the east of St Mary's porch is a grave known as 'The witch's grave'. It has a skull and crossbones device carved into it, and is marked with the name 'Nutter', as are several other graves in the churchyard. Contrary to popular opinion, it is unlikely that this is the last resting place of the Pendle witch, Alice Nutter. The date of death of the occupant has worn away, but none of the other gravestones in the churchyard date back to 1612 when the execution of Alice Nutter took place at Lancaster. Even if this grave pre-dates the others, it was the accepted practice to burn witches bodies after hanging, or else to bury them in un-consecrated graves.

Bull Hole Farm

Bull Hole Farm was the home of a branch of the Nutter family for many years. It was here that John Nutter gave a dish of cows' milk to the witch Chattox and her daughter Elizabeth. After receiving the milk with very little gratitude, Chattox poured it into a can across which she placed two sticks prior to chanting a spell over it.

John Nutter's son took offence at this and kicked over the can, spilling the contents whereupon the old witch hurled insults and curses at him. The next day one of Nutter's cows became sick and died less than a week later.

Tynedale Farm

Tynedale Farm dates from the middle of the eighteenth century, although there was another building at the site prior to this. The earlier farm would have been the one that allegedly played host to coven meetings of the Pendle Witches.

There have long been tales of ghostly activity at Tynedale, including a phantom monk who kneels to pray by the roadside and a woman, possibly a servant, who haunts the area dressed in a long cape and a skullcap.

When a team from Living TV's *Most Haunted* programme visited the farm at Halloween 2004, psychic medium Derek Acorah claimed to sense the presence of nine witches there. The crew held a séance during which several members of the camera crew suffered breathing difficulties and became unwell. The presenter, Yvette Fielding, felt as though something was choking her and after the cameras stopped rolling she screamed at the ghosts. Witnesses claimed that the glass they were using for divination then flew across the room and shattered on the ground, as the table tipped over, its legs apparently torn from their sockets.

The team's experiences at Tynedale surprised the current owners of the farm, Norman and Ruth Nutter, who allowed them to film there. They are currently renovating the property, which they have known for a long time and Ruth told me that the house has a pleasant, serene feel to it and she loves to be there.

NOGGARTH

Lower Well Head Farm

Lower Well Head Farm dates back to the 1500s and like its neighbour, Tynedale Farm; it was a meeting place for the Pendle witches and their coven. It is probable that at one time, the farmhouse served as a morgue and the adjacent pathway bears the name 'Corpse Way'.

Hollow footsteps regularly walk across the empty upstairs rooms of the building, especially at around six-o-clock on Saturday evenings.

The crew from *Most Haunted* also visited Lower Well Head Farm on the same night that they filmed goings-on at Tynedale (Halloween 2004). Derek Acorah claimed to have picked up the presence of a spirit called Edward at Lower Well Head and that of a witch whose face kept changing.

A sign at Tynedale.

Tynedale Farm, scene of a 2004 visit by Living TV's *Most Haunted*.

OSBALDESTON

Osbaldeston Hall stands on the south bank of the River Ribble. There has been a building on the site since a man called Oswald erected his home there in Anglo-Saxon times. In the fourteenth century, it belonged to the Countess of Lincoln, widow of Earl Henry de Lacy and later, during the Tudor period, the Osbaldeston family found favour with the monarchy, and were able to extend and modernise the old hall. The house once boasted a great hall, two wings, and a moat. It is now an equestrian centre.

One of the rooms in the old hall, known as the Court Room, had several dark red stains, which generations of inhabitants were unable to obliterate and were generally considered to be the blood of a murdered guest.

The story goes that one evening many members of the Osbaldeston family gathered at the house for a great feast. During the liquor-laden meal, an argument broke out between Thomas Osbaldeston and his brother-in-law. They agreed to fight a duel to settle the disagreement, but their anxious relatives stopped this. Later the two antagonists met, by accident, and Thomas drew his sword, thrusting it deep into the other man's breast, spilling his blood on the floorboards.

Thomas was punished by having his land taken from him and his murdered kinsman periodically returns to the room to seek revenge. He moves around the murder room with his arms uplifted, whilst blood flows from his wounded chest. The stains were finally lost in 1946 when the old wood was replaced.

The Red Monk and the Blue Lady

Osbaldeston also boasts two more ghosts, about which there is little information. One appears to be a red monk from the Anglo-Saxon period, when Ailsi, son of Hugh, owned the house and monks cultivated the land. The other is the spectre of a woman who floats through the rooms wearing a long blue gown. Both these ghosts are of a friendly, unthreatening nature.

PADIHAM

The Red Rock

The Red Rock pub at Heightside stands in an area formerly known as North Town, on the road between Padiham and Sabden. It first appears listed as an 'ale house' in the early nineteenth century when it was the end cottage of three, but the building probably dates back to the seventeenth century. In its early days as an alehouse, it seems to have had several generations of the same family as tenants.

The current owners, Jackie and Lawrence Neil, have been at the pub since 2004 and, like other landlords before them, they have witnessed a series of spooky goings-on. Jackie, who did not believe in ghosts before moving to the Red Rock, appears to be especially sensitive to the pub's spirit guests and has had several encounters with them.

She told me that shortly after moving in to the pub, they began to renovate the public rooms. One day, as Jackie was standing in the doorway between the dining room, which used to be part of the middle cottage, and the bar, she felt somebody brush firmly past her. She thought it was her son and was about to reprimand him when she turned and saw him up a ladder at the far side of the room. When she told her husband about her experience, he commented that she had probably had a 'muscle spasm'. Jackie accepted the explanation, not really wanting to think otherwise.

However, as the Neils continued with the renovations it seemed as though they were disturbing the incumbent ghosts, who did not like the intrusion. Jackie came out of the ladies' toilet one day and saw the greyish-brown figure of a woman standing in the doorway. The woman did not appear to have a face and disappeared as quickly as she had appeared, but Jackie is in no doubt of what she witnessed.

One of the bar staff also had an odd experience in the ladies' when she heard someone enter the next cubicle and close the door. On leaving the toilets, the barmaid asked who had gone in there, as the pub was almost empty. She was told that no one had moved from their seats at the bar but, when she went back to investigate, the toilets were empty. There is no way out of the building without passing through the bar.

Jackie and members of her kitchen staff have felt 'sympathetic' pats on their shoulders while cooking and the spring-loaded kitchen doors have opened of their own accord.

Lawrence and Jackie's bedroom is above the dining room, and Jackie has woken on more than one occasion to the sound of children playing and chattering nearby. She told me that the voices seem to come from the walls, but when she has looked out of the window, there has never been anyone on the isolated road outside. A study that Lawrence commissioned from the University of Central Lancashire refers to there being several children living at Heightside in the 1851 census, but they do not appear in the census record of ten years later, although the family name remains the same.

Lawrence told me that Fred, who was landlord at the pub in the late 1980s and early 1990s, had corroborated the couple's eerie experiences. Fred had four dogs, two of which had the run of the public rooms after closing time. One night Fred had heard the dogs growling, so he

The Red Rock Inn, Padiham.

Does this well at the inn hold its own secret?

went downstairs to investigate. He found the doors secure, but in one room something odd had happened – the eight bulbs and shades from the cartwheel ceiling light had been removed and were stacked neatly in opposite corners of the room.

Another licensee at the Red Rock, Alma Thompson, sought help in the pages of the *Lancashire Evening Telegraph* in February 2003, because she was curious to learn more about a ghost whom the locals had called Mary. She claimed that Mary was responsible for glasses flying from shelves, appliances switching themselves on and off and other unexplained phenomena.

The Yorkshire ghost hunters 'In-Search-Of-Spirit' visited the Red Rock in early 2005, and confirmed that they could sense several spirit energies especially that of a woman from the 1860s named Mary and a child of seven or eight years old called Margaret.

The Neils told me that they do not feel frightened or threatened by their ghostly housemates, but Lawrence is a little worried that a filled-in well in the pub car park may contain the remains of an executed witch – but maybe that is another story!

The Padiham Witch

Margaret Pearson from Padiham, stood trial alongside Old Demdike, Chattox and the rest of the Pendle witches at Lancaster Castle in 1612.

She did not hang with her associates, however, but was sentenced to stand in the pillory at Clitheroe on four successive market days, followed by a year's imprisonment.

Mrs Sagar's Return

The Clitheroe Times for Friday 19 August 1898 carried a long and complicated ghost story that ended with the reporter carrying out research that was beyond the normal call of duty.

The report began by telling how a large crowd had begun to gather each night outside number one Pitt Street, off Pendle Street, waiting for something to happen. It described the house as a 'tenement' that faced the front of Padiham's Mount Zion Baptist chapel. The tenants at the time, a tackler at Commercial Mill and his family, had only lived at the address for ten weeks, and were 'flitting' because of the strange things they had witnessed there.

Shortly after moving to Pitt Street, they had begun to be disturbed at night by strange noises downstairs. The husband had got up to investigate on several occasions but had found nothing untoward, so he had assumed that it was his neighbours 'making mischief' for his family because they were newcomers to the town. On Padiham Fair (a local holiday) 'the unmistakable form of a woman' appeared in the couple's bedroom, where after crossing and re-crossing the room between the fireplace and the wardrobe it disappeared. The apparition continued to show itself both in the bedroom and downstairs, where it usually came out of a closet. The tackler's wife told how all members of the family had either seen the woman at sometime, or had heard her climbing the stairs, making the bare wooden steps 'groan and creak as if an ordinary person was walking on them.'

One night the husband waited on a sofa in the kitchen until the ghost made her appearance, and asked her if she wished 'to communicate anything'. The spirit did not reply, but had raised her hand slightly, walked into the scullery, came back to the foot of the stairs and vanished.

The family eventually told their neighbours of these ghostly visits, describing the woman to them in detail. They all agreed that the description fitted Mrs Sagar, a 'devout and somewhat eccentric' woman who had lived in the house until her death three years before. Her son had drowned himself in the Lowerhouse Print works lodge, aged thirty, and following an acrimonious split in the congregation of her local Baptist Church Mrs Sagar had become so agitated that she suffered a stroke and died. Following her sudden demise, no-one had stayed in the house for long and the tackler's family quickly followed suit and found new accommodation.

The reporter was so intrigued with the tale that he decided to investigate further and, together with a group of friends, went to the empty house just before midnight. They crouched in a corner of the dark kitchen and waited for something to happen. After about half- an-hour, they heard a sound coming from upstairs 'like the sudden dropping of a Venetian blind' and expected to hear footsteps creaking down the stairs. Instead, there was a thudding on the door and four policemen came in, waving their lanterns to check what was going on. After they left, satisfied with the explanations they received, the dispirited ghost-hunters gave up their vigil and went home to bed.

The men returned to Pitt Street the next night hoping for better results and were not disappointed. The clatter of a dropping blind echoed through the house once more, but this time there followed the sound of heavy furniture scraping across the bedroom floor. They heard footsteps coming down the stairs and everyone expected to see the ghost of Mrs Sagar enter the room. When she failed to materialise, they lit candles and went upstairs to see if someone was up there. They found no one, and there was no sign of a Venetian blind, or any furniture at all that could have accounted for the noises they had heard. The men were sure that they had witnessed a ghost and that they had not been the victims of a prankster. As the reporter notes at the end of his story, 'One person may be deceived or even two, but the fact that ten or eleven were present puts such a thing quite out of the court in this case.'

PENDLE HILL

The Pendle Witches

In August 1612, ten so-called witches from the countryside around Pendle Hill stood trial at Lancaster assizes accused of practising the black arts. Seven were found guilty and hanged: two were found not guilty and hanged: and one, Alice Grey of Colne (whose trial was not recorded) was acquitted.

Those condemned to die were: Jane Bulcock (not guilty), John Bulcock (Jane's son, also not guilty), Anne Whittle (Chattox), Anne Redfearn (daughter of Chattox), Alice Nutter, Katherine Hewitt (Mouldheels), Elizabeth Device (Old Demdike's daughter, known as Squinting Lizzie), James Device (Old Demdike's grandson), Alison Device (Old Demdike's granddaughter). Elizabeth Southern (Old Demdike) died in Lancaster gaol before the trial began, and so avoided the ordeal and subsequent hanging that her fellow Pendle Witches suffered.

The story of the Pendle Witches begins with a feud between the Southern family, of whom Old Demdike was the matriarch and the family of Anne Whittle, (formerly Chadwick) usually called Chattox. Both Demdike and Chattox were women in their eighties by the time they were arrested and the ill will between them had festered for years. Matters finally came to a head when Bessie Whittle, a daughter of Chattox, stole some food and clothing from Old Demdike's home at Malkin Tower. Alison Device discovered the culprit wearing some of the stolen clothes and reported the theft to the local Justice of the Peace, Roger Nowell of Read hall. Nowell questioned Bessie and sentenced her to a term in Lancaster castle, causing the two families to begin accusing each other of every crime they could think of, including witchcraft.

On 18 March 1612 John Law, a pedlar travelling towards Colne, refused to open his backpack to look for pins for Alison Device. Alison cursed him for his obstinacy, whereupon he had a seizure and fell down at her feet. Other travellers discovered him and took him to the nearest alehouse to recover, where his son, Abraham, found him three days later. John had recovered enough to tell his son that Alison had bewitched him with a curse and the last thing he could remember before becoming unconscious was seeing a big black dog with fiery eyes standing by her side. Abraham found Alison and dragged her to his father's bedside, where she dropped to her knees, crying for the pedlar to forgive her.

Not satisfied with her repentance, Abraham reported her misdeed to Roger Nowell, who summoned her to appear before him at Read Hall on 30 March. When questioned by Nowell, Alison admitted to causing the pedlar's stroke by witchcraft, admitting also that the fierce black dog was her familiar. She blamed her grandmother, Demdike, for making her into a witch and claimed that the Chattox family were also witches. Nowell kept her in custody, then ordered that the two old matriarchs, Demdike and Chattox, be taken to Ashlar House in Fence, so that he could get to the bottom of the accusation and free his area from 'witches'.

On 2 April, Old Demdike, Chattox and Chattox's daughter Anne Redfearn underwent the Justice's interrogation. Demdike confessed to being a witch, claiming that the Devil had first come to her disguised as a boy named Tibb, who later changed into a dog, which sucked blood from her body for nourishment. She admitted killing a child whose father owed money to her daughter, then went on to describe how the quickest way of killing someone was to make a picture of clay, which should be pricked with thorns or pins and then burnt.

Pendle Hill.

Isolated Pendle farms, where the witches may have begged for food.

Pendle Hill, showing a witch on a broomstick that appeared on its slopes for a while in the early 1980s. (John Davitt)

Nowell next examined her old adversary Chattox who, not wanting to appear in any way inferior to Old Demdike also admitted to witchcraft. Chattox told how Demdike had initiated her into the cult fourteen years earlier, since when she had acquired a familiar called 'Fancie' and had met with the Devil several times.

Anne Redfearn was accused of causing the deaths of a spurned suitor, Robert Nutter, and his father Christopher. The witnesses against her in this charge were Robert's siblings John Nutter and Margaret Crooke who convinced Nowell of her guilt. He sent the three women to Lancaster gaol, along with Alison Device who was still in his custody.

The Justice of the Peace had thought this to be an end to the matter but he was informed that there was to be a 'witches' sabbat' at Malkin Tower on Good Friday (10 April), where the two families were going to hatch a plot to free the prisoners and murder the gaoler. Nowell sent Henry Hargreaves to investigate and the young yeoman/constable questioned Demdike's grandson, James Device, who showed him some human teeth, which he claimed had been dug up from the churchyard at Newchurch to be used in spell-making at the sabbat.

Amongst those attending this meeting at Malkin Tower were Elizabeth and Alison Device, who were questioned, along with James, by Nowell and another magistrate, Nicholas Bannister of Altham. Besides confessing to several murders by witchcraft, the three went on to implicate Alice Nutter, John and Jane Bulcock, Katherine Hewitt, and Alice Grey. All were sent to join the rest of their 'coven' at Lancaster, and underwent torture and ill-treatment before the trial took place between 17 and 19 August 1612.

During the trial, the accused did not have anyone to speak in their defence, and when the inevitable verdict came, nine of the Pendle Witches (plus Isobel Roby, who had a separate trial) were taken to a place called Golgotha, on the moors about a mile from the castle, and hanged.

Apron-full Hill

The road across the southern end of Pendle Hill between Sabden and Clitheroe was a route used by traders and their packhorses in days gone by, as they wended their way through the forest of Pendle. Known locally as 'The Nick o' Pendle', it is said to derive its name from a giant called Owd Nick who once roamed the area. The giant became angry and gathering up some boulders from the hill overlooking the road, (now called Apronful or Apron-full Hill) he stood atop the crag and hurled them at Clitheroe Castle. One of the stones hit its mark and made a hole in the wall of the keep, but Owd Nick's apron strings broke and the boulders spilled down the slope, forming the rocky landscape.

One version of this tale has the giant then trundling angrily towards Sabden, where he made the marks in the ground known as the Devil's footprints.

Jeppe Knave

High on the ridge that stretches from the top of Pendle Hill towards Whalley is a burial mound, which historians now believe to date back to the Bronze Age, and may have contained the body of a tribal leader before looters got at it.

A centuries old local legend however, names it as The Jeppe Knave Grave, after a criminal from Norman times who outraged the villagers of Wiswell and Pendleton with his blatant flouting of the laws of the time. One version of the legend says that a housemaid killed Jeppe during a robbery and another that the law-abiding country folk caught and hanged him for his crimes. Whatever the cause of his death, neither village would allow the burial of his remains on their land. After much discussion, and many arguments they buried him on the ridge – half way between their boundaries.

Jeppe's ghost reputedly walks unceasingly between the two villages, looking for further mischief to perform.

Wild and windswept crags at the top of Pendle Hill.

Robin Goodfellow's Well

One of the most mystical places on Pendle Hill is a well lying close to the top of the 'Big End' and known as either Robin Hood's well or Robin Goodfellow's well. Some say that there used to be a stone cross marking the spot and that it was an old place of Christian pilgrimage, but it is likely that it was first a pagan site used in the worship of water spirits.

The well has been suggested as a meeting place for the Pendle Witches but there is no evidence to confirm this, although it is almost certain that they would have known of its existence.

The Wandering Monk

A ghost of a monk, which some say resembles Abbot John Paslew, has often been sighted in the lanes around Pendle Hill.

In 1959, a girl from Hurst Green told how, along with her friend, she had seen a hooded monk as they drove along the Nick-of-Pendle road at 10 o'clock one Friday night in March. The brown-cloaked figure was standing stock still at the side of the winding road and the girls had to swerve to avoid a collision. When they looked back to see what had happened, the road was empty.

On another Friday night in 1966, again at 10 pm, a young couple were travelling along the road from Sabden to Clitheroe when the girl yelled out in fright. She had seen a tall man, who was wearing a long dark robe and whose hood hid his face, standing by the hedge. Her boyfriend saw nothing as he was concentrating on the dark lane, although he did admit that his companion appeared visibly shaken by the incident.

Other sightings have placed the ghostly monk along the length and breadth of Pendle Hill, but whether it is the spirit of the same wandering monk or several different apparitions is open to debate.

REEDLEY HALLOWS

Reedley Hallows has connections with the witch, Chattox who used to visit John and Robert Nutter at Laund House. The two men were Roman Catholic priests who felt forced to hide their calling during the days of the anti-Catholic persecution.

The Oakleigh Spectre

Businessman and shop owner Abraham Altham built Oakleigh in 1883, as his private residence. During the first half of the twentieth century, it functioned as local government offices and headquarters. In the 1980s, a hotel chain bought it and have since made many modifications and extensions to the beautiful building.

Staff members at The Oaks, as it is now named, have reported seeing an apparition of a young woman wearing a long white gown, which rustles as she glides between rooms in the old parts of the house.

They believe that the girl was a maid in the Altham's household many years ago and because she becomes a more frequent visitor during building work or alterations, she may not be comfortable with changes being made to her home.

The Oaks Hotel, formerly Oakleigh.

RIBCHESTER

The Romans built a fort at Bremetenacum, now known as Ribchester, to guard the junction of two of their major roads. The old church and churchyard now cover most of the site, but the museum contains a good many relics.

The White Bull Ghosts

The White Bull, situated in the heart of Ribchester, bears a stone plaque with the date 1707. This date refers to the old section of the pub, which was originally a courthouse, although the discovery of a medieval wattle and daub wall during recent renovations seems to provide evidence of an earlier building. The magnificent Tuscan pillars that guard the front door are thought by some to be relics from Ribchester's well-documented Roman ruins, and the crudely fashioned figure of a white bull fixed to the front façade was erected sometime in the eighteenth century.

Until fairly recently, shackles used to detain prisoners were still fixed to the wall, and local legend says that two of the prisoners who died in the cellar whilst awaiting 'justice' in the late 1700s were children.

Emily Keen, who along with her husband Jason took over the pub in 2004, describes herself as 'a sceptic' who did not believe in ghosts until she began to experience strange goings-on at her new home. She recounted how she has witnessed beer pumps in the cellar switch on and off without satisfactory explanations and told me that she saw the figure of a small man dressed in blue emerge from a wall, cross a ground floor corridor and disappear through the cellar door. The chef, Mark also had a terrifying experience when he woke up one night with the feeling that someone was holding his arms in a menacing way.

Emily also told me that her regular customers often see a ghost, who they know as 'Old Jack', sitting in the corner of the poolroom, which used to be part of the stable block serving the courthouse. The room was not converted to this usage until the 1940s, and 'Old Jack' wears clothes from the post second world war era.

When a former landlady decided to use the pool table area as a dining room it seemed that her actions upset the old man as the lights kept failing, the room was often very cold and the customers did not like using the room as they said it felt 'creepy'. When she reinstated the pool table, the lights behaved once more.

The Boggart of Hothersall Hall

The ownership of much of the land around Hothersall is traceable to the ancestors of the Hothersall family as far back as the twelfth century. Adam de Hothersall, a staunch upholder of Catholicism, lived on his estate on the North bank of the River Ribble in the fourteenth century, then, in the mid-nineteenth century, Sir James Openshaw, a wealthy industrialist, pulled down the old building and built a gothic mansion in its stead. Simon and Emma Watts bought and refurbished the hall in 1998.

An old legend surrounding the hall tells of a boggart that tried to persuade a local man to sell his soul to the Devil in exchange for three wishes. The man agreed, but being of a crafty nature, he spent his wishes wisely: First, he wished for wealth, then for happiness, and his third wish was that the boggart should spin a rope from the sands of the River Ribble. The man also insisted that the boggart must agree to be buried under a nearby laurel tree if he failed, thus hoping that the spirit would be unable to complete the bargain and carry him off to the Devil.

The boggart, confidant in his supernatural abilities, agreed to the terms and began to spin, but each time his rope was nearing completion the man poured water over it, causing it to disintegrate. Eventually, worn out with effort and realising he had been duped, the boggart agreed to remain buried amongst the roots of the great tree for as long as the tree was alive.

Above: Tuscan pillars said to be from Ribchester's Roman ruins guard the doorway of the White Bull.

Right: The inn's eighteenth-century figure of a white bull.

This gruesome head is said to be the petrified head of the Hothersall boggart.

Several years ago, a man dug up a grotesque stone head in the area and it was rumoured that this was the petrified head of the Hothersall Boggart. The head now lodges in the fork of a tree at the gate of the Hothersall home farm and appears to glare down in anger and frustration at all who pass by.

ROUGHLEE

Roughlee nestles at the foot of Pendle hill following the contours of Pendle Water. It lies at the heart of Pendle Witch country and must have been familiar to all of them.

Roughlee Hall

It seems to be W. Harrison Ainsworth who placed Alice Nutter at the Elizabethan hall of Roughlee, in his novel *Lancashire Witches: A Romance of Pendle Forest*. Potts, who wrote an account of the Lancaster witchcraft trials of 1612 as they occurred, described her as being a rich woman, previously of good character, but does not give her address.

Gladys Whittaker, in her twentieth-century publication *Roughlee Hall, Fact and Fiction* is of the opinion that it is unlikely that Alice Nutter ever lived at the hall and that local legend may have confused her with Helen Hartley, who is recorded as mistress there at the time. Whittaker suggests that she may have been the widow of a yeoman, and as such would have been of a status more inclined to have contact with Old Demdike, Chattox and their like.

Alice Nutter, who may possibly have lived at a farmhouse in the same village, remained silent throughout her trial. The assizes at Lancaster found her guilty of killing Henry Mitton of Roughlee by witchcraft, and her hanging took place on 20 August 1612, at the same time as a number of her co-accused.

SABDEN

The Devil's Footprints

Craggs farm clings to the slope of Pendle Hill just above the village of Sabden. In amongst a large pile of sandstone rocks on the farmland is one, which according to tradition, bears the imprint of the Devil's feet. The two prints lie side by side and measure roughly two feet long by six inches wide, and are supposed to mark the spot where Satan landed on Pendle to meet with a coven of witches.

The White Hart Boggart

According to Cheryl Hindle, who along with her partner Shawn McCullough, has tenanted Sabden's White Hart since 2004; the pub has a mischievous spirit with a penchant for throwing things.

Cheryl and her bar-staff have had close shaves when glasses have flown off shelves, not just dropping to the floor but also lurching sideways before crashing to the ground with some force. Customers have also witnessed glasses shattering behind the bar when no staff members were present. Cheryl told me that things often go missing from the same area, only to turn up weeks later in very unlikely places. One side of the bar has sudden inexplicable drops in temperature and the landlady sometimes senses the presence of an older woman watching her as she goes about her daily chores.

She informed me that at one time the cellar of the pub used to be a morgue and has a very eerie feel to it. On occasion, the beer pumps have suddenly stopped working, and either she or

Roughlee Hall. (courtesy of Lancashire Library and Information Services)

The White Hart at Sabden.

Shawn has gone down to the cellar to find the gas pumps turned off, although no one has had access to them. The handle that controls the gas needs turning upwards to achieve this, so it is not possible for the pumps to switch off accidentally.

Cheryl and Shawn are now used to living with their boggart, and are quite comfortable with its mischief.

SAMLESBURY HALL

Samlesbury Hall, on the banks of the River Ribble, is now a museum, gallery and antiques centre run by the charitable trust that saved the old manor from dereliction in the 1920s.

Samlesbury Hall - home to several ghosts.

Gilbert de Southworth built the oldest part of the hall in 1320, following his marriage to Alice D'Ewyas. It was subsequently improved and added to by succeeding generations of the family. It is reputed to have several ghosts but, like most haunted houses with a long history, the exact identities of the ghosts are subject to conflicting theories.

The White Lady

The White Lady is generally accepted to be the ghost of Lady Dorothy Southworth, a daughter of Squire Sir John Southworth, who was Sheriff of Lancashire in 1562 and a devout Roman Catholic and, it seems, something of a bigot. The young Dorothy fell in love with a knight from a neighbouring wealthy Protestant family. Her father discovered the affair and forbade it, so the young lovers plotted an elopement. On the appointed night, the young swain, accompanied by two trusted friends, came to Samlesbury Hall to collect his bride. Dorothy's brother became suspicious and followed his sister as she kept the tryst. He killed her suitor and his friends in a bloody swordfight and buried them in the domestic chapel.

The Squire banished Lady Dorothy to a continental convent where, traumatised by the loss of her lover, she went mad. After her death, she returned to Samlesbury Hall to look for him and her spectre passes along the gallery, along the corridors and into the grounds where she crouches over the young man's lifeless body. Others have seen her walking with her knight to the spot where the killings took place, where they embrace before disappearing skyward amidst despairing wails.

There have also been suggestions that Dorothy was the name of John Southworth's sister, not his daughter and the White Lady may be the spirit of a recorded daughter, Mary Southworth, who married a Protestant vicar.

Courtyard to rear of Samlesbury Hall where the ill-fated lovers may have secretly met.

Whatever her identity, the White Lady continues to wander Samlesbury Hall and its environs. In recent years, there have been several sightings, including one by a local bus driver who stopped outside the hall to pick up a 'pale lady' who entered the bus and promptly vanished.

The Haunted Gallery

In 1862, following a period when the hall was used as a boarding school for young ladies, it was bought by Joseph Harrison. During renovation work, he discovered three skeletons amongst the foundations, which may have been the remains of the unfortunate young man and his friends from the tale of the White Lady. Harrison had an expensive lifestyle, which led to his bankruptcy. He shot himself in 1878 and his ghost frequents the gallery above the great hall.

The Priest

It seems that Joseph Harrison may have company in the gallery, in the form of a phantom priest. During the Henry VIII's abolition of the monasteries, Samlesbury Hall had several 'priest holes' where Roman Catholic priests were hidden from the wrath of the king. The abolitionists found one of these priests, dragged him from his hiding place and hacked him to death. In recent years, some visitors to the hall have claimed to experience severe shortage of breath in both the gallery and the priest hole and burglar alarms have a nasty habit of ringing when they are switched off.

The Samlesbury Witches

The Samlesbury witches also stood trial at Lancaster in 1612 under the 1604 Witchcraft Act that decreed that the death penalty should be given to 'those who use, practise, or exercise any witchcraft charm of sorcery whereby any person shall be killed, destroyed, wasted, pined or lamed in his body.'

The group of eight, which for some reason included Alice Gray – a Pendle witch, stood trial under a different judge, but unlike their Pendle counterparts, they refused to confess to the trumped-up charges professing their innocence throughout alleged torture and bitter character assassination.

The charges against the Samlesbury defendants Jennet Bierly, Ellen Bierly, Jane Southworth, John Ramsden, Elizabeth Astley, Isabel Sidegraves and Laurence Hay, included murder, grave robbery and cannibalism. Their main accuser was Grace Sowerbutts, the granddaughter of Jennet Bierley and niece of Ellen Bierley. The fourteen-year-old girl told the assizes that she had seen her grandmother turn herself into a black dog, and had been present when Jennet and Eileen had killed a young child by thrusting a nail into its navel and sucking the baby's life-blood through the wound. After the child had died and been buried, Grace said that they had dug up the body and boiled it in a pot. They then ate some for supper and rendered the rest into ointment, which they claimed would help them change form.

The presiding judge had some knowledge of local politics and was aware that local Catholic dignitaries had plotted revenge on those like the 'witches' who had turned away from the Roman Catholic faith. His harsh questioning of Grace caused her to breakdown and admits that she was lying and those she accused were given a 'not guilty' verdict, and went free.

There are no written reports of the trials of the rest of the Samlesbury witches, other than a record that they too were proven innocent of any charges.

SOUGH

The Old Lady of Sough

In January 1965, judo expert Barry Clifton was staying with a friend, Harry Ramsbottom, at his cottage in Colne Road, Sough. The men were living on the ground floor as Mr Ramsbottom had not been there long and had yet to decorate the bedrooms, which he was using for storage.

One evening Barry went upstairs to get a case that he needed and had almost reached the landing when a pair of black, buttoned boots came into his eye-line. He quickly became aware that an elderly, white-haired woman, wearing a black skirt and stockings, occupied the boots. A white blouse and starched pinafore completed her outfit. Barry noticed that the woman had a cameo brooch, suspended on a long black ribbon around her neck and was about to speak to her when he realised that he and Harry were the only people in the house at the time. He let out a shout and jumped most of the way back down the staircase, landing so heavily that his foot went through the bottom step.

According to Harry Ramsbottom, Barry was not a man who frightened easily but he felt terrified by what he had seen and sat by the fire for the rest of the evening, shivering and shaking despite the warmth. Barry again saw the ghost on the staircase a few days later, when she spoke to him. He was uncertain what she had said, but reported that he was not so frightened on this occasion as he was expecting her to re-appear at some point.

Although Mr Ramsbottom had not seen the woman himself, he told how the door at the bottom of the stairs kept opening of its own volition despite having a firm 'sneck', which should have ensured that it could not blow open.

Mr and Mrs Banks, previous tenants of the cottage, backed up the two men's stories and Mrs Banks admitted to having seen an old lady, dressed as Barry had described, in one of the bedrooms when she had lived there.

Towneley Hall.

The Boggart Bridge.

A well at Towneley, where
the children of the family
loved to play.

TOWNELEY

Towneley Hall was home to the Towneley family for over five hundred years, until they sold it to Burnley Corporation in 1901. It became a museum two years later.

The Towneleys were staunch Roman Catholics and evidence of their continued allegiance to their faith during the period of Catholic persecution can be seen in the elaborate chapel alterpiece and the priest hole.

The Boggart beneath the Bridge

Legend says that long ago a malicious boggart used to live under a bridge on the Towneley estate. It would lay in wait for travellers and then leap out to taunt and terrify any who crossed the bridge. As the boggarts antics worsened, the locals persuaded the Towneley priest to go and 'lay' the spirit.

The boggart, however, proved more than a match for the churchman and he would only promise to return to the spirit world providing he could return for one day each year. The priest agreed to this and the boggart vowed to keep his word for as long as green leaves grew by the bridge.

When the troublesome spirit had returned to its rightful world, the local people planted evergreen holly bushes on the banks of the stream to prevent the boggart reneging on his promise and this is how the area took the name 'Hollinhey Clough.' Perhaps the boggart still visits the area once a year, but no one seems to know on which day to expect him.

The Regretful Spectre

John Towneley was born in 1473 at Towneley Hall, his family home and he accepted a knighthood when he became Sheriff of Lancashire. As a younger man, John gained permission from the king to increase the size of his Towneley estate and enclose the boundaries. In order to do this, he hired henchman to evict the local peasants from the cottages they had built on common land, causing much hardship and suffering. Towards the end of his life, he came to regret his callous actions and was plagued by guilt until he died in 1541.

After his death his spirit began to materialise every seventh year to warn his successors to repair the damage he had done, chanting a verse that began, 'Lay out; Lay out, Harelaw and Hollinhey Clough.' In other words, he was telling them to open up the enclosed land and return it to the people.

One version of the legend says that when John Towneley's spectre makes its appearance he requires that there is a sudden death in the locality, although if John is returning because of a guilty conscience over his past demeanours it is hard to see why he would make such a demand.

Lady O'Hagan

Lady Alice O'Hagan was the last of the Towneley family to inhabit the ancestral home. It seems that she abandoned it even after death, choosing instead to haunt the area known as 'The Summit', which is at the top of Burnley's Manchester road. She is reputedly seen driving her pony and trap along the winding road and as she careers along the horses' hooves sound to be pounding along a pebbled surface, although the road was asphalted many years ago.

TRAWDEN

The Sun Inn

In 1976, when renovations were taking place at the Sun Inn Trawden, the removal of old plasterwork on an interior wall revealed a date stone for 1793. The inn, originally built as a row of weavers' cottages, must have witnessed many dramas over the last couple of centuries.

The Sun Inn, Trawden.

When Wayne Forster and Faye Medcalfe took over the running of the Sun Inn in 2005 and they have already had several experiences that they cannot explain.

On their first night on the premises, Wayne sat downstairs a while after he had locked up. As he mused over his day, he heard a sturdy door latch lift and fall followed by strange shuffling noises. Wayne put this down to the building 'settling' and thought no more of it until a few weeks later.

On this occasion, Wayne had prepared the pub for the evening opening and then gone upstairs to shower and change. This took him about thirty minutes so he was surprised to come down and find the kettle boiling on the shelf behind the bar. He checked to see if someone had come in, but the door was locked and he was still alone. As Wayne pointed out, if he had accidentally switched on the kettle before going to shower, (and he was sure he had not) it would have boiled dry in thirty minutes, and it had been almost full when he found it.

On another occasion, Faye was readying the function room for an event when she heard footsteps coming down the corridor from the bar. She heard the sound of someone coughing and choking, so went to investigate. She found no-one. Faye admits to feeling 'spooked'. The next day she was discussing the subject with Wayne and two customers when the hand-drier in the ladies' toilet (which is just off the corridor) suddenly began to work. The machine is an old push button type that does not function automatically, but no women were in the inn, nor had there been all evening.

The Phantom Poacher

In the first half of the twentieth century, a Trawden man was walking home from work late one dark night and took his usual short cut through the cemetery He saw a strange eerie glow and, although he was frightened, he crept from headstone to headstone across the graves to see what the light could be.

Graves in Trawden churchyard, where 'Old Truman' used to catch rabbits..

In the top corner of the graveyard, he saw a man who was holding a candle and moving a large pile of stones one by one. He asked the man what he was doing and as the figure turned, and replied that he was flushing out a rabbit that he had tried to shoot earlier, he recognised him as Old Truman, the poacher, who had died some time before.

The Ghostly Carriage
In the late twentieth century, two schoolgirls stood transfixed when a horse-drawn carriage appeared in front of them near to Trawden rubbish dump. The silent apparition moved swiftly down the road before disappearing as they watched.

WHALLEY

Standing on the banks of the river Calder, Whalley has been a place of Christian worship for more than a thousand years and is mentioned in the Doomsday Book.

The Celtic Crosses
The churchyard at Whalley contains three mysterious crosses, which the monks who used to live at the Abbey ascribed to either St Augustin or Paulinus, but which other experts have theorised, date back long before their times, probably to the tenth century. A local tradition has it that anyone who is able to translate the hieroglyphic markings on the largest of the crosses will be endowed with the power to become invisible at will. Harrison Ainsworth weaves this myth into the fabric of his book about the Lancashire Witches.

The Abbot's ghost

Cistercian monks moved to Whalley Abbey in 1296, from their former monastery in Stanlow, Cheshire, but did not finish its construction until the end of the fourteenth century. The last Abbot of Whalley was John Paslew, who was born in nearby Wiswell and studied for a degree in divinity at Oxford University.

When, in 1537, Henry VIII demanded that all his subjects swear an Oath of Allegiance and claimed the riches of the Church for himself, Abbot Paslew refused to give up the abbey to the king, or to take the oath. The courts found him guilty of high treason and executed him in March of that year. Although records seem to point to his execution taking place near Lancaster Castle, local legend has it that he was hanged close to his beloved abbey and buried in Whalley churchyard, where there is still a gravestone which some believe is from the abbot's tomb. This gravestone is at the centre of a curse which was laid upon the Assheton family, now of Downham, when they bought the property from the Crown in 1553. The curse stated that if any member of the family should step on Paslew's grave they would die within a year.

Celtic cross, Whalley churchyard.

The ghost of Abbot Paslew has been seen many times since then, floating through the ruined cloisters, sometimes accompanied by a procession of chanting monks. Part of the abbey is now a residential conference centre owned by the Diocese of Blackburn, and there have been regular reports of ghostly footsteps echoing round the impressive building.

Horace

According to the *Clitheroe Advertiser and Times* of 17 May 1968, The Duckworth family had acquired a sitting tenant when they moved into Abbey Croft four years previously. 'Horace' as they called the ghost, first made himself known to their daughter, Carolyn, when she heard him climbing the stairs in the house next door. It seemed odd to her, as she knew that the staircase in that house was nowhere near the adjoining wall, which was, in any case, at least two feet thick. On another occasion, Mrs Duckworth was with Carolyn in the living room when a sports trophy rose and levitated above the television set before crashing to the floor.

Following this incident, Horace became increasingly active and the family were very aware of, though not frightened by, his presence. One evening, the Duckworth's son Darren, aged twenty-four, felt the floor vibrating under his feet. The silent but rhythmical pounding continued for quite a while, as though someone or something was trying to come up into the room. Abbey Croft had no cellars and the floors were stone flags covered by composition flooring.

The ghost's last reported manifestation was during a party at the house when at least two of the guests saw a cloaked and hooded figure in the garden. The guests claimed to have heard the wind rustling through the monk-like figure's garments on an otherwise breezeless night and were unaware that Abbey Croft's original use was as an alehouse for the abbey's resident monks and weary travellers.

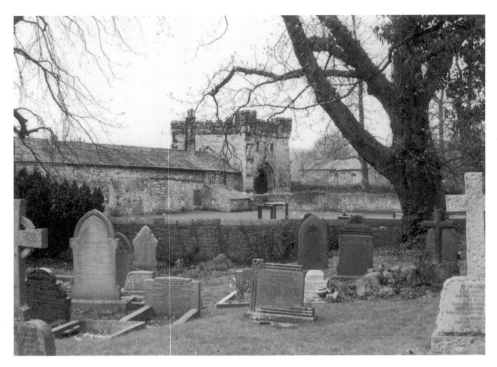

Whalley Abbey from the graveyard.

Old stone coffin at Whalley church.

The occupiers of the other houses in the block never saw or heard Horace, but the owner of the house next door to the Duckworths explained that his staircase had been moved from its former position against their wall during earlier renovations.

The White Lady of Whalley

A team of local filmmakers reported feeling an eerie presence, other than that of John Paslew, at Whalley Abbey whilst they were filming there. The presenter and the camera crew got more than they had bargained for when they felt that someone or something was watching them. As the crew checked out the situation, they saw an intense white flash at the window of a room, which staff had informed them was empty.

They believed that they might have witnessed the ghost of the White Lady, the wife of Ralph Assheton, whose family had bought the abbey from the king following the dissolution of the monasteries. She is usually sighted standing by the fireplace in the main hall, often when the weather is particularly cold.

WHEATLEY LANE

Hoarstones

In 1633, Edmund Robinson, an eleven-year-old boy from Wheatley Lane, accused a group of his neighbours of witchcraft. The boy told two Justices of the Peace, Richard Shuttleworth and John Starkey, the following tale when they interviewed him at Padiham. Edmund claimed that he had been out gathering wild plums one evening, when he saw two greyhounds in a meadow. One was black, the other brown and both had golden strings attached to their collars. Thinking that he recognised the dogs as those belonging to Mr Nutter and Mr Robinson the lad took hold of the strings, deciding to abandon his search for plums and with the dogs' help catch a hare or two for the pot.

The hounds however refused to co-operate and when they failed to chase a hare that he flushed out, Edmund beat them both with a large stick. The boy claimed that at this point the black dog changed into Mrs Dickinson and the brown one into a small boy whom he did not recognise. Mrs Dickinson offered him a silver shilling if he would agree not to tell any one about this, but Edmund replied that he would denounce her for a witch. On hearing this, the woman took a bridle from around her waist and threw it over the strange boy, who had taken the form of a white horse. Then, pulling Edmund onto its back with her, she galloped to a large house called Hoarstones.

Edmund went on to describe the things he had witnessed at Hoarstones, including men and women drinking and carousing together, eating lumps of seared meat which they pulled down from the ceiling with a series of ropes and seeing three old crones take clay images from the beams and stick thorns into them. He escaped from his captor as she joined in with the antics, and ran, greatly distressed, to tell his father what he had seen.

As a result of Edmund's story, a jury at Lancaster found seventeen suspects guilty of witchcraft. They did not hang, however, and a report of the trial reached the King's Privy Council who ordered that four of the witches should undergo examination at Greenwich. The four were Jennett Hargreaves, Frances Dickinson, Mary Spencer and Margaret Johnson.

The medical jury who examined these women declared that they could find nothing 'unnatural', such as a third nipple, on any of them, even though Margaret Johnson confessed to practising witchcraft. It is unclear what happened to the accused following this declaration, but there is no account of an execution of witches taking place around this time.

The Bay Horse at Worsthorne.

WORSTHORNE

Old Jam Well

There is supposedly a well in the village of Worsthorne, which used to supply most of the dwellings with drinking water. Known as 'Old Jam Well' it is reputed to have been the haunt of fairies in times past.

The fairies would milk the village cows during the night, and make tiny pats of butter. Some of the villagers claimed to have found these butter-pats by the well, and some even told of seeing the fairy folk amongst the cows in the pasture. They generally described the men fairies as being decked out in green jackets and fairy women as wearing white stockings.

Old Thrutch

There was an inn at Worsthorne called The Bay Horse long before the building of the present day hostelry of that name.

Over three hundred years ago, the landlord of the inn also had a corn mill near Swinden reservoir, which he ran with the aid of his wife. She was a thrifty, somewhat greedy woman who saved every penny she could and stashed it away, not telling her husband of its whereabouts, or even its existence.

One stormy winter's night the woman slipped as she crossed the river on her way home from the mill and the swollen torrent swept her away to her death. Rumours of her hidden cache reached her bereaved husband, but he could not find any trace of it and eventually dismissed the tale as idle gossip.

As time elapsed, strange noises and ghostly sightings beset the inn. The villagers believed that the landlady had returned in spirit to collect her money and, as the hauntings became more frequent, the landlord decided he had had enough and bricked up the room at the centre of the visitations.

Things went quiet after this until the beginning of the nineteenth century when a landlord known as 'Old Johnny o' th' Tayleurs' took over the inn and reopened the bricked up room. The ghost, thus released from its holding place, began to appear every night. She wore a brown silk dress and developed a habit of removing the bedclothes from the landlord's children's bed as they slept.

Late one evening, a group of quarrymen and labourers were drinking at the inn when one went to visit the outside privy. On his return, he could not open the door, even though he put all his weight against it. As he wrestled with it, he heard a hollow voice instructing him to 'thrutch' (push). The man, angry by now, replied, 'Thrutch the Devil, thee thrutch and I'll pull!'

At this, the door flew open and as the labourer fell inside, he heard the rustle of a long silk skirt sweeping along the corridor, but saw no one.

The door to the haunted room was bricked up once more and the ghost, who was given the nickname 'Old Thrutch' after this last incident, was never seen again.

WYCOLLER

A settlement has existed at Wycoller since before 1000 BC. It was an agricultural community until the introduction of the woollen handloom in the eighteenth century. In the 1890s, people left the hamlet when the Water Board planned to build a reservoir on the land.

The ruins of sixteenth-century Wycoller Hall.

This never came about as they found a well, but Wycoller had only its ghosts for inhabitants until comparatively recent redevelopment and restoration.

The Hartley family built Wycoller Hall in the sixteenth century, but several generations of the Cunliffe family were its main inhabitants. It is the house described as 'Ferndean Manor', the home of Mr Rochester in Charlotte Brontë's book *Jane Eyre*. It was still standing at the beginning of the twentieth century, but it is now a ruin with at least two ghosts.

The Spectral Horseman

The spectre of a horseman returns to Wycoller each year, on a wet and windy winter's night. His horse gallops furiously across the ancient Pack Horse Bridge and stops at the front of the hall. The ghost, dressed in typical Stuart costume, then leaps from his mount, flings open the door, and climbs the now vanished oak staircase to the upper floor. The terrified screams and tortured groans of a woman resound in the howling wind and then the horseman remounts and gallops back over the bridge from whence he came.

This annual happening is reputedly the re-enactment of the murder of one of the Cunliffe wives, whose husband retuned home one evening to find her embracing another man. Cunliffe presumed he had been cuckolded and killed his wife on the spot. It later transpired that the lover was the woman's long lost brother, but there is no mention in the tale of what happened to him.

Black Bess

Bess was the wife of Simon Cunliffe, another squire of Wycoller Hall. During a hunt, the fox headed in through the open front door and ran up the stairs seeking cover. He was followed by

A spectral horseman is said to gallop across this pack-horse bridge.

Remains of stone staircase at Wycoller Hall.

the squire, his baying hounds and the rest of the hunt. Bess, who was at the top of the staircase, was so terrified that she screamed and spooked the horses. Simon was furious at this and raised his crop to hit his wife. Bess dropped dead at his feet and now appears in the stiff black dress that she was wearing at the time.

Fred Bannister in *The Annals of Trawden* claims that this woman in black was, in fact, a black woman that one of the Cunliffes married in the West Indies. On the way back to England, he decided that it would not be a good idea to take his bride home to Wycoller and tossed her overboard. Bannister says that she is the black Bess who appears at the hall, searching for her murderous husband.

On the other hand, J. Carr writes in his *Annals and Stories of Colne and Neighbourhood* (1878) that it is 'Old Bess', the murdered wife of the cuckolded 'Spectre Horseman', who appears in Wycoller, in her black silk dress 'when all is hushed and still'.

Guytrash Padfoot

Guytrash Padfoot, sometimes known as Skriker, is the spirit of a large-eyed black dog who patrols the country paths and lanes around Wycoller. His appearance or the sound of his shrieking howls are reputed to herald a local death.

AFTERWORD

I have never seen a ghost, nor would I wish to. The nearest I have come to a 'spooky experience' was many years ago when I was having a bad time of things and my mother's silver thimble appeared in my bed one morning. My mother had been dead for several years and, as far as I knew, the thimble had been in her workbox, which was stored at the back of a downstairs cupboard full of junk. I stopped trying to work out 'how?' and just took comfort in the thought that my mother was perhaps trying to confirm that she was still there for me, as she had always been.

However, whilst researching this book, I have spoken to many sane and sensible individuals who claim to have had ghostly encounters and I have no reason to doubt their sincerity or perception.

As the Bard himself says: 'There are more things in heaven and earth, Horatio, than are dreamt of in your philosophy' (*Hamlet*: Act 1 scene 5).

You must make up your own mind.